D1239216

FOCUS ON MATTHEW

a study guide for
groups & individuals

revised edition

by
Carol Cheney Donahoe

© 1990, 2001, by Living the Good News
All rights reserved
Printed in the United States of America

No part of this book may be reproduced or transmitted in any
form or by any means, electronic or mechanical, including
photocopy, recording or any information storage and retrieval
system, without permission in writing from the publisher.

Formerly published as *Focus on the Gospel of Matthew*.

Living the Good News
    a division of The Morehouse Group
Editorial Offices
600 Grant, Suite 400
Denver, CO 80203

Cover design: Jim Lemons
Interior design: Polly Christensen

The scripture quotations contained herein are from the *New
Revised Standard Version Bible*, copyright © 1989 by the Division of
Christian Education of the National Council of the Churches of
Christ, in the USA. Used by permission.

ISBN 1-889108-69-3

Contents

Introduction to the Series v

Introduction to The Gospel of Matthew ix

Matthew 1—4
The Coming of the Messiah 1

Matthew 5—7
The Teaching of the Messiah 17

Matthew 8:1—11:1
Messianic Ministry and Mission 35

Matthew 11:2—12:50
Opposition and Response 49

Matthew 13:1-52
Seeing and Hearing the Messiah 63

Matthew 13:53—16:20
The Messiah Revealed 74

Matthew 16:21—18:35
Following the Messiah 88

Matthew 19—20
Journey to Jerusalem 100

Matthew 21—23
The Messiah's Authority 113

Matthew 24—25
The Vision of Things to Come 127

Matthew 26:1—27:26
The Last Supper, Arrest and Trial 140

Matthew 27:27—28:20
Crucifixion, Resurrection and Commission 152

Bibliography 164

Introduction to the Focus Series

THE FOCUS BIBLE STUDY SERIES offers a unique and inviting way to interact with and experience God's word, allowing that word to filter into every area of life. It is designed to challenge growing Christians to explore scripture and expand their understanding of God's call. Each volume echoes the **Living the Good News** strategy of experiential learning; that is, they welcome the participant into a journey of discovery.

Journal Format

Focus Bibles Studies are adaptable for individual use or group use. Adult classes, small-faith communities, midweek Bible studies and neighborhood discussion groups will find these books a helpful resource for in-depth exploration, personal growth and community building. When used in a group, leadership may be designated or shared.

Each of the book's twelve sections begins with a brief synopsis of the passage and a *Find the Facts* section, which can help you prepare to consider the material. Informative commentary is not intended to provide definitive answers to the meaning of the passage, but to give you background information, clues to the context and suggestions for thought. It can serve as a point of departure for personal reflection or group discussion.

The questions posed in each section are designed to speak to at a variety of levels:

- Some are questions of *interpretation:* What is the author's meaning in this passage?

- Some are questions of *application:* How does the author's message apply to contemporary Christianity?

- Some are questions of *reflection:* How is this God's message to me? to my family? to our community?

Every level contributes to the faith-nurturing impact of the study. The variety of questions are grouped together topically so that you can respond to the level most directly pertaining to your situation. The same goes for group use: participants can respond to those questions most relevant to their current circumstance.

Each section includes suggested *Group Activities*. These activities provide small groups with experiential activities that can help participants to grasp an idea through various methods of learning rather than through intellect alone. These activities involve the whole person—senses, emotions, mind and spirit. If you are using this study in a group setting, we encourage you to incorporate these activities into your group's time together. Many adults may feel awkward when invited to work with clay or pipe cleaners, or to create songs or poetry; they may feel these are childish activities. Such concrete experiences, however, can serve to move group members from learning *about* an idea toward an *understanding* of the idea.

Each section closes with a *Journal Meditation* and a *Stepstone to Prayer*. These offer you the opportunity to record or illustrate thoughts and feelings about the passage explored and to express these to God in prayer. The *Journal Meditation* invites you into deep, personal reflection that can produce life-changing understanding. *Stepstone to Prayer* leads you into a time of communion with God.

Individual Use

- Begin each session with prayer—that you will be open to God's message to you, that the Spirit will illuminate God's work, and that you will be empowered to follow God's call.

- Read the passage several times in the scripture translation of your choice. (Note that the New Revised Standard Version Bible has been used in the preparation of these studies.) Try to understand what the author is saying before you begin to interpret, apply or reflect on the message.

- Note key words or phrases that you find especially significant in the scripture. When you have finished a section, go back and review these words or phrases and explore their importance in light of your greater understanding of the passage.

- Spread your exploration of any given section over several days; come back to those question that have provoked considerable thought. You may be surprised at the new insights you find if you spend some time each day on the passage. Give the passage time to sink into your heart and mind.

- Record your thoughts in the space provided. The discipline of journaling can help you synthesize your thoughts and direct your understanding.

Small Group Use

- Prepare for each gathering following the suggestions given above under "Individual Use." Group interaction is impoverished if participants have not immersed themselves in the passage before meeting.

- Begin your time together with prayer. Expect God to increase your faith, expand your understanding of scripture and build your fellowship.

- Accept one another's experiences and interpretations of the passage. Listen carefully to comments; offer your own insights; be willing to look at things in new ways.

Small Group Leadership

- Prepare for each gathering as a participant first. Your role as a leader is not to teach but to facilitate the process of sharing and discovery for everyone.

- Keep in mind the group's time restraints. Begin and end on time. Underline those questions that you think will be most appropriate for your group's discussion time, but be open to those questions that group members wish to pursue.

- Choose one or two group activities that your group will enjoy and learn from. Make sure you have gathered any required materials for your chosen group activities.

- Begin and close each gathering with prayer. Ask a volunteer to read each section of the passage as you come to it in the study.

- Welcome all contributions, but keep the discussion on track. Certain passages may have two or three possible interpretations. Do not be concerned if all participants do not agree in their understanding. Acknowledge the differences of opinion and move on to the next question.

- Allow time at the end of each gathering for those individuals who wish to share their thoughts or drawings from their *Journal Meditations*.

- If your group members are not well-acquainted, it may take some time to build a trust level within the group. Let the dynamics of the group develop as group members gain confidence in themselves and in one another.

Introduction to the Gospel of Matthew

READING AND STUDYING the Gospel of Matthew launches us on a voyage into "good news." *Gospel*, from the Greek word *evangelion*, literally means good news. By the third century, the four gospel writers, Matthew, Mark, Luke and John, had become known as "evangelists," bearers of the good news.

From the moment that the two Marys rushed away from Jesus' empty tomb to tell the other disciples the good news, people have continued to share the story. The women told their friends; the friends announced it to gathered groups. Word spread and, as believers banded together to build their lives on the good news of Jesus, the Church grew.

Over time the stories of Jesus crystallized, achieving some stability in the details included and the words used as Christians told and retold them. Eventually Jesus' followers wrote down these stories. People collected them and put them together to form cohesive written accounts of the heart of the good news—the life, death and resurrection of Jesus the Christ.

The four gospel writers do not present the story of Jesus in the same way. Each reflects a unique viewpoint. Each presents a different order of events in Jesus' life. Each uses the materials available to him to address the needs and concerns of his special audience. All, however, proclaim the same good news.

The gospels do not report "news" in the sense of a newspaper story written to give a precise account of events. Instead, we must dig to establish the "who, what, where, when, why and how" of these ancient writings. We then discover the central purpose of each gospel writer: to testify to the incredible good news—the birth, life, death and resurrection of Jesus—and its implications for humanity.

Date and Authorship

Part of the long debate over the authorship of Matthew hinges on the similarities seen in the gospels of Matthew, Mark and Luke. Clearly, the similarities are strong enough to suggest that all three books are linked to common sources. Matthew has included most of Mark, though the stories are shortened to leave room for Matthew's original material, consisting mainly of Jesus' teachings.

Tradition assumes that the book was authored by the apostle of the same name, Matthew the tax collector, mentioned in MATTHEW 9:9 and 10:3. This hypothesis, however, fails to explain why Matthew, an apostolic author, would rely so much on Mark, who was a non-apostolic author. Why would Matthew not rely on his own, firsthand remembrances?

Another theory suggests that the original material found in Matthew may have been the written reflections of the apostle Matthew, recorded originally in Aramaic, a Jewish dialect. A later unknown compiler may then have combined the writings with the stories found in the Gospel of Mark to create a new gospel written in Greek. Matthew's name would be associated with this new gospel because his Aramaic writings provided a portion of the text as well as its overall viewpoint.

Whatever position one holds, it seem unlikely that the apostle Matthew actually wrote the original Greek document that we now know as the Gospel of Matthew. Presumably, however, some of the apostle's personal experiences and memories of Jesus' ministry live on in the book we are about to study. In this study the name Matthew refers to Matthew, the Evangelist.

The dating of Matthew is equally difficult. Some scholars choose a date as early as A.D. 60, some as late as A.D. 90–95. Many are comfortable with a date sometime between A.D. 70 and A.D. 80. It is safe to say the Greek Gospel of Matthew, the translation of which we use today, probably appeared about forty years after the death and resurrection of Jesus.

Setting

The destruction of Jerusalem and the temple of the Romans in A.D. 70 triggered a crisis for the Jewish people of Matthew's time. The Jewish religious community suddenly found itself fighting for its existence, and in that fight, returning to a Jewish orthodoxy that, in its homogeneity, offered a better chance of spiritual survival. Such orthodoxy, however, tolerated much less diversity, and the Christian Jews found themselves no longer accepted as a Jewish sect. They stood separated from their previous Jewish identity. The temple crisis ended an era for Judaism and aggravated the polarization of Christians and Jews.

For Jewish Christians, the destruction of the temple and the threat to Judaism also threatened their continuity with their sacred past. For them Jesus was the Messiah, the fulfillment of God's promise to Israel. If Judaism could crumble, what did that mean for the Messiah? Their own roots seemed uncertain.

So Matthew writes for a people in transition, for a Church with an uncertain future. He wants to offer continuity with the past and confidence for the future. He writes to show the Jewish Christians that their true link to the past rests, not in the traditional structures of Judaism, which seem to be passing, but in the great promise of Judaism: the coming of the Messiah.

Scribes, Pharisees and Sadducees figure prominently in Matthew's gospel. Scribes could read and write Hebrew and, as successors to the prophets and sages, specialized in religious questions. They guarded the written tradition carefully, resulting in a legalistic perspective with a tendency to restrict knowledge to the initiated (Mt. 7:29; 23:23).

The Sadducees represented the aristocracy and the priesthood. Prior to the destruction of the temple in A.D. 70, they dominated the Sanhedrin, the highest Jewish governing body. But the Sanhedrin was abolished when the temple was destroyed, and following A.D. 70 the Sadducees rapidly lost power. The Sadducees believed that only the written Torah, the first five books of the Bible, was binding for the Jewish people.

The Pharisees, by contrast, believed that all of the Jewish law was binding for the Jews. Devoted to the law and its interpretation, the Pharisees resented Jesus who spoke on his own authority. Matthew portrays them as Jesus' chief opponents, which may reflect Matthew's experience of the growing hostility between Christians and Jews after A.D. 70. The Pharisees may also have been angered by how closely much of Jesus' teaching followed their own, while at many points it soundly condemned their hypocrisy (Mt. 23:3).

Major Themes

Matthew's gospel reveals Jesus as the Messiah, the fulfillment of Old Testament prophecy. Matthew designs his gospel to teach and guide the Jewish Christian church of his time. Interestingly, of the four gospel writers, only Matthew uses the Greek word *ekklesia* (church); Matthew offers guidance for the worship, ethics and missionary activity of the Church.

In spite of Matthew's essential Jewishness, his gospel stresses the universal mission of Christ. Jesus comes not only as the Jewish Messiah, but as the Messiah for all people.

Matthew writes to convince his Jewish readers of the legitimacy of Jesus' messiahship in the light of the Old Testament and to assure his Jewish Christian readers that belief in Jesus did not mean that they were abandoning true faith, but rather that they were accepting its fulfillment. The events of Jesus' life, death and resurrection stand solidly as part of God's dealings with people throughout time, dealings that continue as a reality in our lives today. Just as many Jewish believers needed to hear again that God is the God of all people, so we today need to remember that God's kingdom extends far beyond our familiar cultural limits to all the world.

Structure

The arrangement of Matthew's material reflects the work of a skilled author whose careful combination of stories and teachings communicates the book's themes. The Gospel of Matthew divides easily into three parts:

- first, an introduction (chaps. 1–2)

- second, the body, which tells of Jesus' ministry (chaps. 3–25)

- third, the conclusion, telling of the death and resurrection of Jesus and the commissioning of the disciples (chaps. 26–28)

The body (chaps. 3–25) subdivides into five sections, each containing a narrative (story) portion and a discourse (teaching) portion. Matthew uses a formula (or some variation of it) to end each of these sections: "Now when Jesus had finished saying these things..." (7:28; 11:1; 13:53; 19:1; 26:1).

The teaching of Jesus stands centrally in Matthew's gospel. Through this teaching, the Church finds practical guidelines for life and worship. Fittingly, Matthew concludes the gospel with the challenge of the great commission, the Church's task for the present and future.

Matthew 1–4
The Coming of the Messiah

OUR FIRST STUDY IN MATTHEW covers several major events: Jesus' birth, his baptism, his temptation and the beginning of his ministry. Though we may wish for more biographical details, Matthew's intent is to present the Messiah; he thus devotes most of the book to Jesus' ministry and message. Read the first four chapters of MATTHEW, watching for hints of important themes:

- Jesus as Messiah

- the fulfillment of God's purpose in history

- Jesus as the Messiah to both Jews and non-Jews

- Jesus in conflict with religious leaders

- Jesus and the message of the kingdom

Find The Facts

Who is the main character? How is he introduced? Where is he born? How does he get to Nazareth? What is the first recorded event of his adult life? What happens to Jesus in the wilderness? When and where does he begin to preach? Who are the first disciples? What are the major aspects of Jesus' ministry?

Consider:

1. Make a simple outline of the important segments of the first four chapters of Matthew. Give titles to the various sections.

2. What is important about the birth of Jesus according to Matthew? What seems most significant about the visit of the wise men from the East?

3. What role does John the Baptist play? Describe his personality. Why do you think he became so popular with the people?

4. What events prepare Jesus for his ministry? In what way does each event add to Jesus' understanding of his calling?

Matthew 1:1-25

Before launching into the main body of his work, the story of Jesus' public ministry and teaching, Matthew sets the scene by describing the background and birth of Jesus. Matthew establishes Jesus' credentials by identifying Jesus both theologically and genealogically in the first verse. He introduces Jesus as the Christ (Heb. *Messiah*) and traces his family tree back through David, the king from whose line the Messiah was expected, to Abraham, the traditional father of the nation of Israel (GEN. 12:2-3).

Matthew's inclusion of this genealogy tells us at the outset that he sees Jesus as the fulfillment of God's promises as recorded in the Old Testament.

The modern mind can have some difficulties when faced with the failure of the names to agree with the Old Testament or with the genealogy of Jesus as recorded by Luke (LK. 3:23-38), but historical accuracy is not the point. Common practice allowed the telescoping of genealogies to achieve a desired effect. Luke's genealogy is traditionally considered to reflect Mary's ancestry, not Joseph's. Matthew includes the genealogical information as testimony to his faith that all of history, beginning with the patriarch Abraham, has culminated in the fulfillment of God's purpose in the person of Jesus, the long-awaited Messiah. The status of Jesus as the legal son of Joseph, a descendant of

David, is more important to Matthew than the virgin birth. Neither the conception nor the birth are recounted here, only their consequences.

Matthew declares that the birth of Jesus is no ordinary affair and he again stresses the connection to Old Testament prophecy (1:18-25; Is. 7:14). God is now with us.

Matthew tells this story from the point of view of Joseph, a just and obedient man (1:19, 24). Though distressed by his betrothed's pregnancy, he plans to divorce her quietly without bringing charges that could lead to a death sentence. The name *Jesus* (1:21, 25), the Greek form of *Joshua*, was common; the name means Savior or "Yahweh saves." Note that Matthew, interested in making clear the identity of Jesus, includes this information and prepares the reader for the climax of the story.

Consider:

5. *Why is Matthew so careful to provide Jesus with impeccable credentials? What would the relationship to David and to Abraham have meant to Matthew's Jewish audience? What does viewing God as active and intentional in human history mean to us today?*

6. In contrast to the account in Luke 1:26-38, which focuses on Mary, Matthew's account of the events leading up to Jesus' birth focuses on Joseph's reactions. In what ways can you identify with Joseph's dilemma? What do you think enabled him to respond with obedience in what must have been a somewhat disturbing situation? What helps you continue in faith when the facts seem contradictory?

7. What does it mean to "save his people from their sins"? Who are his people? In what sense do you think of Jesus as Savior?

Matthew 2:1-12

Chapter 2 continues with signs of Jesus' identity as the Messiah. The New Revised Standard Version translates the word *magi* as "wise men," but the term means something more like "astrologers." Magi believed that a star would announce the arrival of a great human being.

As the only gospel that tells the story of the visit of the magi, Matthew makes a special point by including the story. Over time, Jews had come to identify the star "out of Jacob" with the anticipated Messiah (Num. 24:17). Again Matthew insists that Jesus is the fulfillment of Old Testament prophecy (Mic. 5:2). There seem to be two other major points:

- The birth of Jesus is a cosmic event (signified by the star).

- The birth is important not only for Jews but for all people. (See Mt. 28:19.) Non-Jews, the magi, come to worship Jesus at the very beginning; today the Church celebrates this event as the feast of the Epiphany.

The birth also has political implications; Herod is troubled by the news (2:3). (Herod the Great ruled in Palestine until his death in 4 B.C.) We can imagine he was even more distressed when the chief scribes and priests found a prophecy to confirm the magi's story. Verse 2:6 quotes Micah 5:2. The gifts of the magi (2:11) are royal gifts traditionally interpreted as gold for the King, incense for God, and myrrh for the One who is to die. Myrrh is the resin of an Arabian shrub and produces a pleasant aroma. The magi prove themselves to be wise indeed when they decide to return home by another way (2:12). Note that this is the second time that a dream is important in Matthew (1:20).

Consider:

8. *When you think today of the birth of Jesus, in what ways does it have cosmic implications? universal implications? political implications? How can you relate these to your own life?*

9. As the star directed the magi, what directs you to Jesus? What gifts would you like to offer to Jesus? What do they symbolize?

Matthew 2:13-23

This section describes more events that Matthew interprets in the light of Old Testament prophecies. Note the repetition of the formula, "this was to fulfill..." Verse 15 quotes from HOSEA 11:1; verses 17-18 from JEREMIAH 31:15; the reference in verse 23 is uncertain. Connecting these events in Jesus' life to the Old Testament presents Matthew's view that Jesus does not stand alone as an isolated phenomenon, but rather that Jesus is the completion of a story begun long ago.

Matthew consistently portrays Joseph as faithful and obedient. Three more times the angel of the Lord (an Old Testament phrase for God in visible form) appears to him in a dream (2:13, 19, 22) and gives a command that Joseph follows exactly. God continues to guide the course of events through obedient believers.

This section presents a stark contrast to the preceding material; the divine child, just presented with royal gifts, is forced to flee for his life. Scholars often point out parallels between the story of Israel and Matthew's story of Jesus. Joseph is instructed to go to Egypt, the traditional place of refuge (1 KG. 11:40). Besides foreshadowing the persecution and rejection that Jesus was to encounter as an adult, the story is reminiscent of Moses, Israel's great deliverer. Set adrift on the Nile as an infant in order to elude a king's persecution, Moses later escaped and returned to lead his people.

Consider:

10. Why do you think Matthew is anxious to explain the events of Jesus' life in light of the Old Testament? Is this a useful way today for us to understand scripture? Why or why not?

11. Matthew reports that the angel of the Lord appears to Joseph through dreams. In what ways do we receive messages from God today? Who are the messengers? How can we identify them?

12. What do you think is significant about the several moves that Jesus' family makes during his infancy and early childhood? In your own life, what influence has your hometown had on your lifestyle and values?

Matthew 3:1-17

Time passes, perhaps twenty-five years, between the end of chapter 2 and the beginning of chapter 3. To set the scene for the beginning of the Messiah's adult ministry, Matthew introduces a colorful new character, John the Baptist. Dressed as a desert bedouin (3:4), John preaches a dramatic message of repentance (3:2) and heralds the coming of a mightier one (3:11). John the Baptist paves the way for the Christian message of salvation.

John preaches in the wilderness of Judea (3:1), the mountainous region west of the Dead Sea. Here people gathered to hear the strange new prophet. Many accept his message and are baptized. "Repent" (Gk. "change your mind," Heb. "turn back, change direction") calls the people to come back to the covenant between God and Israel (Ex. 19:3-6). If God's kingdom is "at hand," all God's past activities are coming to fruition. John's baptism is clearly understood as a cleansing, a washing away of sins, but the baptism of the One who is to come is different (3:11). With the advent of Jesus, baptism by water becomes a sign of baptism with the Holy Spirit, the receiving of God's unconditional love. In verses 7-12, John addresses the Pharisees and Sadducees (see Introduction) and accuses them of self-righteousness ill befitting religious leaders. This "brood of vipers" ultimately sees that Jesus is crucified.

Jesus' own baptism takes place after John overcomes an initial reluctance to baptize him. Jesus emerges from the water with a dramatic and powerful new sense of affirmation and self-understanding. Matthew describes a visible event as well: the Spirit of God descends like a dove (for rabbis, a symbol of Israel) and plainly identifies Jesus as the Messiah, "beloved" (meaning also "chosen one").

Consider:

13. *Repentance involves a change of direction. Of what do we need to repent in the Church today? What new directions would lead us into deeper understanding of Jesus the Messiah? In your own life, where do you need to change direction?*

14. *John the Baptist accuses the Jewish leaders of hypocrisy and says their actions do not bear fruit. How might his words have affected the Jewish leadership? the developing Christian Church? What are the dangers of smugness or self-righteousness for church leaders today? for any of us who close our minds and hearts to new ideas?*

15. *If baptism washes away sins, why do you think Jesus wants to be baptized? In what ways do you think it was "fitting" for Jesus to be baptized? What was the result of Jesus' baptism? In what ways did it equip him for ministry?*

Matthew 4:1-11

Immediately after the powerful experience of his baptism, Jesus withdraws into the wilderness to be alone for forty days and forty nights, presumably to reflect on what it means to be the beloved Son of God.

The time Jesus spends in the wilderness parallels Israel's wandering in the wilderness (Num. 14:33-34). To Matthew's Jewish audience this would also recall the receiving of the Ten Commandments by Moses on Mount Sinai (Ex. 34:28) and the receiving of a revelation by Elijah on Mount Horeb (1 Kg. 19:8).

The devil (4:1), the tempter (4:3) and Satan (4:10) are names for the leader of evil forces actively hostile to God. Three temptations follow, each associated with power and each rejected by Jesus with a quotation from Deuteronomy. The first (4:3) may reflect the current belief that the messianic age would bring a miraculous abundance of material goods. Jesus, though hungry, rejects this simple solution to satisfying physical needs (Dt. 8:3).

In 4:5, the devil suggests an even more dramatic way for Jesus to prove he is the Son of God. Cleverly, since Jesus refutes the first suggestion by quoting scripture, the devil in verse 6 quotes Psalm 91:11-12. Jesus also rejects this scheme for impressing people (4:7), again with a quote from scripture (Dt. 6:16). Undaunted, the devil offers political power (4:8). Once again Jesus rejects the easy route to power, certain now of his mission to proclaim a different sort of kingdom, a different sort of power.

16. What words in this passage link the three temptations to the voice from heaven at Jesus' baptism? On what resources does Jesus rely when rejecting power as a way to prove that he is the Son of God? On what resources do you rely when you need to resist a powerful temptation?

17. Why do you think Jesus felt a need to be alone after the experience of baptism? What questions might he have been asking himself? What questions do you have about the nature of your own ministry?

Matthew 4:12-25

The last half of chapter 4 records the beginning of Jesus' public ministry. When he returns from the wilderness he learns that John the Baptist has been arrested (4:12); this news reinforces the theme of unrest and danger that accompanies Jesus' career.

Once again Jesus is on the move; he leaves Nazareth and goes into Galilee, a move Matthew interprets as fulfillment of another prophecy (vv. 15-16 quote Is. 9:1). John's arrest evidently signals Jesus to begin his own preaching (4:17). In verses 18-22 he calls the first of the disciples. For Peter, Andrew, James and John "repentance" means literally turning around or taking a new direction. They leave their fishing nets and follow Jesus.

Verses 23-25 serve as an introduction and summary for the next section of the book of MATTHEW. Chapters 5–9 will describe in detail Jesus' teaching, preaching and healing, a similar summary appearing in 9:35.

Consider:

18. *How do the primary activities of Jesus—teaching, preaching and healing—differ from the activities he rejects in 4:1-11? What are the primary activities of ministry today? In what ways are preaching, teaching and healing still good categories for ministry? How would you describe your own ministry as a baptized Christian?*

19. *What is involved in the response of Peter, Andrew, James and John to Jesus' call? In what ways do we respond to Jesus' call today? What are some characteristics of one who follows Jesus?*

Group Activities

1. Many families today enjoy researching their ancestry and constructing a family tree. Often a family has a coat of arms that shows symbols depicting the history of its name.

   Divide into groups of three or four. Distribute large sheets of paper and various colored markers. Ask each group to design a coat of arms for Jesus by selecting three or four symbols from Matthew's description of Jesus' background and birth.

   Ask the small groups to share their artwork and explain their choices to the whole group.

2. Invite the group to brainstorm answers to this question:
   - Who are the wise people of today (that is, those who are aware of "God with us" in the world)?

Record the group's ideas on newsprint, then discuss:

- What are the characteristics of these wise people? *(for example, willing to risk, searching for truth, open to new signs or information, etc.)*
- Where are they found?
- How do we recognize them?

3. Invite group members to participate in a roleplay of the calling of the disciples. Assign parts for *Jesus, Peter, Andrew, James, John* and *Zebedee,* giving participants a few minutes to get into character. Ask someone else to describe the setting. Suggest that the observers think about what is involved in the call to discipleship.

After the roleplay, ask the *disciples*:

- How did your part in the roleplay feel?
- What were some of your thoughts?
- Did you want to drop everything and go? Why or why not?
- Was it a hard or easy decision?

Ask *Jesus*:

- How did it feel to play your part?
- What were your expectations? Did you expect the disciples to follow you right away? Why or why not?

Ask *Zebedee*:

- How did it feel to play your part?
- What did you think about your sons taking off and leaving you? Why didn't you go, too?

Ask *observers*:

- What insights about the call to discipleship did you have while you watched the roleplay?

Journal Meditation

In many ways verse 1:23 is the heart of Matthew's gospel. Though the quotation (Is. 7:14) speaks of a birth in the time of King Ahaz, for Matthew salvation is just this: God with us. Jesus, Messiah and Savior (1:21), brings this to pass once and for all. Reflect quietly for a few minutes on the meaning of "Emmanuel" for you. Make a list or draw a picture of ways in which you understand God to be with you.

Stepstone To Prayer

God, help me to be aware that you are with me.

Matthew 5–7
The Teaching of the Messiah

CHAPTERS 5–7 MAKE UP the material known as the Sermon on the Mount, one of the most familiar collections of Jesus' teaching. Though the sermon probably represents fragments of Jesus' teaching that were recalled by oral tradition, the gospel writer has organized them carefully. The main body of teaching (5:17–7:12) is preceded by an introductory series of blessings (5:1-16) and followed by a corresponding series of warnings (7:13-27). Read quickly through MATTHEW 5–7.

Find The Facts

Who is speaking to whom? What is the setting for the teaching? What qualities characterize the persons whom Jesus says are blessed? What is Jesus' attitude toward the law? What warnings does Jesus give us? What is the effect of his teaching on the crowds?

1. List some of Jesus' main topics in 5:17–7:13. What seem to be his major concerns?

2. According to the Sermon on the Mount, what are some of the qualities of discipleship? characteristics of the kingdom of heaven?

3. Matthew probably uses the phrase "kingdom of heaven" because of the Jewish tradition that avoids naming God directly. Though to us the word *heaven* may suggest the next world, to Jews it was more like a synonym for God. What does the image of the "kingdom of God" mean to you?

Matthew 5:1-16

In the literature of most major world religions, mountains or high places signify the connection between God and humanity. For Matthew's Jewish audience the fact that Jesus goes up on the mountain to teach (5:1) would recall the sacred image of Sinai, the mountain on which Moses received the Torah (Ex. 19:20). Note also that this gospel concludes with Jesus once again on a mountain (Mt. 28:20). Jesus sits down to teach (5:1-2), assuming the traditional posture of Jewish rabbis while teaching.

Verses 3-12 are known as the Beatitudes, a series of blessings promised to those who seek a right relationship with God and become "the salt of the earth" (5:13) and "the light of the world" (5:14-16). The word *blessed*, which begins each beatitude, is often translated "happy" or "happy is the one who," a formula common in the Old Testament (Dt. 28:1-6; Ps. 1:1). But 5:3-12 is no mere repetition of a formula; Jesus reveals the meaning of true happiness (joy) and calls for a new lifestyle based on a moral revolution that reverses all conventional values like wealth, status and power. The rest of the sermon develops these themes.

Poor in spirit (5:3) may refer to the downtrodden remnant of the people of God (Israel), but carries also a broader meaning of spiritual detachment from material wealth. Comfort for those who mourn (5:4) implies that though suffering is part of life it can lead to blessing. Verse 5:5 echoes the promise of Psalm 37:11. The fourth beatitude (5:6) employs images of hunger and thirst to suggest that our need for God is that basic. Mercy (5:7) is a theme that runs through the gospel; here Jesus indicates we ourselves are to be merciful, not just hope for mercy from God. Pure in heart (5:8) means single-mindedness or integrity. The Greek word *peacemakers* (5:9) was rarely used and usually applied to emperors, those who actively pursue peace. Persecution (5:10) may have already been present in the Church at the time of this writing. Righteousness means to be in right relationship. Verse 11 may refer specifically to the persecuted disciples and the Church.

In Jesus' time, salt (5:13), a valued household item, was salty earth kept in a small cloth bag that was thrown into a pot to lend flavor to the food, then fished out and used over and over until nothing was left but the impurities. For us, the image of salt suggests that which gives flavor and taste. Light (5:14-16) is that which gives direction to ourselves and to others. Note the theme of universality; Christians are salt and light "to the world."

Consider:

4. List the attitudes that Jesus says will bring us blessing (that is, make us happy or joy-filled). Which ones do you desire most in your own life? In what way would having these attitudes or qualities of character make you happier?

5. How do the values represented in the Beatitudes stand in contrast to conventional values and attitudes in our society? How could acting on these values—or with these attitudes—effect change in our world?

6. In what ways does your own Christian community provide salt (flavor, zest) and light (direction, clarity) to the larger community? For whom are you "salt" and "light"? Which people are "salt" and "light" for you?

Matthew 5:17-20

Matthew now turns to a major concern for Jewish followers of Jesus, the relationship of the Messiah's teaching to the Mosaic law. This passage demonstrates that the Messiah who fulfills the prophecy also fulfills the law. The law (and the prophets) comprise the Hebrew scriptures in which God's will is revealed to the people of Israel. Besides the general principles outlined in the Ten Commandments, the written Torah (the first five books of the Old Testament) contains much material on the application of laws to specific situations. To the people of Israel, obedience to the law was a primary demand from God (Dt. 4:1-8) and was expressed through very concrete observances in daily life.

Thus after outlining some startling new values, Jesus is careful to show that his teaching is not contrary to the familiar Mosaic law, but a new interpretation, a perfection of the law as previously understood. The word *fulfill* carries the sense of completion, of accomplishing the purpose or goal that God intended for the law (5:17). Jesus makes it clear that the law is important, and his followers are to take it seriously (5:18-19). Verse 20 brings the new twist. Jesus' followers are to be even more righteous than the scribes and Pharisees, who were understood to be the experts in obeying the law. As Jesus will illustrate in the next several passages, obeying the law is not an end in itself; it is a means of developing the values and attitudes summarized in the Beatitudes.

Consider:

7. *What is the purpose of law (in general)? In what ways do laws reflect the values of a society? What are some of the basic principles behind the laws of your community? your nation? To what extent are these compatible or incompatible with the values outlined in the Beatitudes?*

8. *Besides civil laws, what laws (principles, values) govern your own life? To what extent are these compatible or incompatible with the values outlined in the Beatitudes? How does Jesus himself represent the fulfillment of these values?*

Matthew 5:21-48

This section is a series of illustrations of the Messiah's new approach to the law. They are often called "the antitheses" because each is introduced by the formula, "You have heard that it was said..., but I say to you..." In each case Jesus calls for attitudes that go beyond obeying the letter of the law. To fulfill the law we need to look at more than outward behavior; we need to examine internal attitudes.

The council referred to in verse 22 is the Sanhedrin, the supreme Jewish court. *Insult* (Gk. *raca*) is a vulgar term of abuse, sometimes used by one rabbi in excommunicating another. Verses 21-26 deal with the law against killing. Jesus' interpretation of this law identifies the underlying cause of murder: anger. Verses 23-26 point out that the way to control anger is through reconciliation. Put first things first, Jesus seems to say; relationship are more important than religious practice or legal formalities (5:23-26).

Verses 27-32 deal with the injunction against adultery. Again, Jesus distinguishes between the act and the inward disposition that causes it. Avoiding sexual involvement with another person's spouse is the rule, but Jesus advises control of lustful feelings, thereby getting to the root of the problem (5:27-28).

Jesus often speaks metaphorically to emphasize a point, as in verses 29-30. His reference to maiming oneself emphasizes that we may need to take drastic measures to reject thoughts that lead to sin. Jesus may also be suggesting that broken relationships can cause so much pain that cutting off a hand or plucking out an eye may seem small by comparison.

Jesus' comments on divorce (5:31-32) further reveal his concern for the significance of human relationships. He seems to be saying that marriage is too important to be treated as lightly as the law has come to treat it, allowing divorce for little or no cause.

The law that forbids swearing false oaths (5:33-37) is not faulty, but Jesus logically asserts that swearing of any kind is unnecessary if we practice telling the truth all the time. The word *swear*, used here in the legal sense, means to guarantee the truth of one's words. In verses 38-42 the Messiah calls us to stretch beyond the old (or childish) concept of even retaliation for wrongs. The law (LEV. 24:18-20), in an attempt to prevent escalation of violence, stated a person could retaliate only as much as the wrong done to him, no more. Jesus says forget violence altogether and respond with generosity.

The last section (5:43-48) offers the basis for Jesus' new ethic—God's love for all people. The messianic message, based on love, emphasizes our need to pattern our attitudes after God's attitudes if we are to be God's children (5:45). Jesus extends the old law of love for brother and neighbor (LEV. 19:17-18) to include not only the people in one's own community but also outsiders (5:46-47), building on the theme of Christ's universal mission (5:13-15). Verse 48 concludes the series of antitheses with a call to wholehearted commitment to imitate the loving God.

Consider:

9. *What value do you see in Jesus' advice to actively seek reconciliation with people we may have cause to resent? What happens when we do not? Which beatitude is most closely related to control of angry feelings?*

10. *Segments of today's society seem quite tolerant of extramarital affairs, but Jesus implies that such behavior disrupts relationships and causes confusion and pain. Which attitude most closely matches your own? Why?*

Matthew 6:1-18

The subject now turns to religious duties or personal piety. As with the discussion of religious law, Jesus begins by stating a general principle: Good works are done privately for the love of God, not publicly to attract the attention of other people. Then he gives three specific examples that correspond to the three traditional "good deeds" or "acts of devotion" of Judaism: almsgiving, prayer and fasting. As in the discussion of the law, Jesus is concerned with the inward dimension of these activities.

Verses 2-4 discuss almsgiving, which includes all acts of charity. Jesus assumes his disciples will continue to give alms (always a sacred duty to the Jewish people); his concern is with the manner in which they do it. The hypocrites have degraded the practice by making it a public show. The metaphor of the left hand's ignorance of the right's activity is one of extreme secrecy. Perhaps the passage means, Do not reveal your generosity to even your closest friends. Similarly, prayer is a private affair, having God as its focus, not a human audience (6:5-7). Again Jesus assumes that his disciples practice prayer; verse 5, like 6:2 and 6:16, includes the word *when*. Religious observances and the prayer life are often represented as complex and/or difficult, but verses 7-8 suggest that prayers may be simple and short. The point is: commune with God who already knows what we need.

MATTHEW 6:9-15 contains the most familiar prayer in Christendom. Jesus offers it as a pattern or guide. Addressing God intimately as "Father" would have been a surprising idea to Jews who were accustomed to avoiding the use of God's name. Though prayer may be private, we say "our" Father because we are part of God's family. The prayer continues with petitions involving God's will and our needs. Note that the only one that includes a condition is the petition for forgiveness (6:12). Jesus thus continues to emphasize the significance of human relationships (6:14-15).

The third traditional act of devotion is fasting. Once again Jesus assumes the practice and goes on to examine the motives (6:16-18). Certain fasts, such as the Day of Atonement, were observed by all Jewish people; as individuals, they also undertook fasts as a means of moral or religious discipline. Jesus points to human admiration as the only reward for those who advertise such practice by looking dismal.

Consider:

11. In what ways does identifying with the nature of God (5:48) imply working toward achieving God's purposes (6:10)? How do religious practices equip us to do this? Of the three mentioned here, which do you find most helpful? Why?

12. *What do you think about the advice not to "look dismal" while engaged in religious discipline? What impression would you like to give to those outside the Church today? In what ways does your prayer life bring you joy? In what ways do you communicate that to those around you?*

Matthew 6:19-34

Concerned about things that distract us from our true purpose, Jesus now focuses on personal values. Jewish rabbis of Jesus' time used the phrase "riches in heaven" to mean good works stored up on account. Verse 21 makes it clear Jesus speaks, not of some future heavenly reward, but of where our hearts are in the here and now.

The sixth beatitude (5:8) promises that those with pure hearts will "see" God. Light is symbolic of being able to find our way; it enables us to see where we are going. Jesus turns the image inward to indicate that we need light within so that we can clearly identify our true values.

Verse 24, another call for purity of heart, explains that to "see" God we must be clear about our priorities. *Mammon*, in rabbinic literature, refers to "money, wealth, profit."

Verse 25 acknowledges that these radical ideas of Jesus are anxiety-provoking. Jesus urges us to counter anxious feelings with trustful attitudes. He gives two examples (6:26, 28) as reassurance that God values and cares for all creation; then Jesus affirms that God places special value on human creatures. Verses 32-33 emphasize that Jesus is talking about getting priorities straight. Food and clothing are necessary but not our most fundamental need. Verse 34 is a reminder that life will always include problems, but one who trusts God will live in the present and not anticipate future trouble.

Consider:

13. Reread verses 25-34 and underline the number of times Jesus tells us not to be anxious. In what ways does anxiety distract us from our true priorities? How does it prevent our seeing clearly? How does anxiety relate to being overly concerned with laying up "treasures on earth"?

14. What treasure do you value most profoundly? How consistent is it with seeking first God's kingdom and God's righteousness? Which of your priorities need to be reordered?

Matthew 7:1-12

Throughout the Sermon on the Mount we note a dual emphasis: righteousness (right relationship with God) implies right relationship with other people. Chapter 7 begins with a focus on this dimension. Jesus urges his followers not to judge others, that is, not to condemn others self-righteously. To condemn others opens us to receiving such condemnation. We are to treat others with the fairness with which we want to be treated. The principle of "measure for measure" (v. 2), borrowed from the world of commerce, illustrates this need for fairness (LEV. 19:35-36; DT. 24:13-16).

Verses 3-5 again use the language of seeing (6:22). Though it is easier to see the faults of others than to see our own, Jesus says to look within, getting our own values and priorities straight. In verse 6, after urging tolerance and compassion, Jesus cautions that respect and discernment for the gospel message itself also have their place. The good news deserves not to be trampled.

Verses 7-11 encourage prayer and picture God as a loving parent. At first reading, the passage seems to promise that God will literally give sincere seekers anything they wish for. If we interpret the passage in terms of its context, we note that Jesus assumes that what we seek is God's kingdom and righteousness (6:33). This is not an easy task, but Jesus here assures followers that a loving God will always respond with generous help to those who truly seek to straighten out their priorities. Verse 12, the end of the main body of the sermon, reminds us again of the two-way nature of righteousness; the route to good relationships with other people is to treat them as we want to be treated. However, the basis for love and kindness to one another is not mere reciprocity, but response to the loving God who treats humanity with such generous love.

15. *How difficult is it for you to give up the principal of fair judgment for one of nonjudgment? How is this related to the ease with which we identify flaws in other people? In what ways do you find it freeing to forget about the flaws of others? How does forgetting flaws help us to avoid self-deception?*

16. *In your own words explain how 7:12 represents a summary of the law and the prophets as interpreted by Jesus in 5:17–7:11?*

Matthew 7:13-28

The conclusion to the sermon begins with warnings that correspond structurally to the introductory blessings. Verse 13 begins a series of paired images. There are two gates, one narrow, one wide; two ways, one hard, one easy; two kinds of trees and two kinds of fruit; and, finally, two kinds of house builders. The series builds up a sense of urgency around the need for a decisive response to Jesus' message.

This section of the sermon includes the familiar theme of putting words into action and also its corollary that actions or "fruits" are the clues to the inner nature of the person. Verses 24-27 illustrate that word and deed are one and suggest that true discipleship means absorbing Jesus' message to such an extent that one's whole life is based on that solid foundation.

Verse 28a is Matthew's formula for indicating that a major discourse is concluded and the narrative about to resume. (See Mt. 11:1; 13:53; 19:1; 26:1.) Here, Matthew includes a comment about the powerful effect of Jesus' teaching on his listeners, the "crowds." Scholars have debated whether the stringent demands of the teachings apply to everyone or only to the inner circle of committed disciples (5:1). The crowds in 8:28 react in astonishment because Jesus speaks on his own authority, whereas their usual teachers, the scribes, teach through reference to traditional authority.

17. What are some of the "narrow gates" you have chosen in your own life? How did these choices help you to grow in understanding yourself? other people? God?

18. Thinking back over chapters 5–7, what are some of the elements of a firm foundation on which to build our lives? How can we strengthen them? Where do you find the greatest stability in your life now?

Group Activities

1. Ask a team of volunteers to defend the proposition, *Happy are the pure in heart, for they shall see God*, using as evidence material from the Sermon on the Mount (Mt. 5–7). Provide pencils and paper and give the team a few minutes to confer.

   The rest of the group may serve as judges. Ask the judges to explain why the case is convincing or why it is not. While the first group prepares its presentation, remaining group members may wish to decide by what criteria they will judge.

2. Divide into groups of three or four and ask each group to dramatize a passage from the Sermon on the Mount. Themes could be reconciliation (5:23 or 25), false prophets (7:15), or serving two masters (6:24), etc. Encourage groups to be imaginative and invent their own story to illustrate the point. When the larger group has reassembled, watch the skits and try to guess which passage is being illustrated. Ask the presenters to explain their choices.

3. Brainstorm associations with the images of light and salt. List these on newsprint, whiteboard or chalkboard. Discuss:
   • How is the world today in need of these things?
   • In what ways can Christians be salt and light for the world?
   • How is this done in our congregation? in our individual lives?

4. Divide into group of three or four and give each group newsprint and markers. In the small groups discuss:
   • In what ways do we understand fasting, almsgiving and prayer as necessary "acts of devotion" or "good works" for religious people today? List on chalkboard, whiteboard or newsprint.
   • What are some other activities that enhance or express our life with God?

   After a few minutes, invite groups to share their lists. Ask:
   • What do our lists have in common?
   • In what ways do these various activities enhance or express our religious values?

Journal Meditation

Reflect again upon Emmanuel (God with us). Which of Jesus' teachings in the Sermon on the Mount contribute most to your understanding of how God is with you? List or draw pictures of the ways in which these teachings help you see God in your life.

Stepstone To Prayer

God, help me to see clearly enough to seek first you kingdom and your righteousness...

Matthew 8:1–11:1
Messianic Ministry and Mission

C HAPTERS 8 AND 9 describe Jesus' ministry in Galilee. In chapter 10 Jesus instructs the disciples about their mission. If the previous section, the Sermon on the Mount, can be considered a presentation of the Messiah of the Word, the teaching Messiah, then this section is complementary, portraying the Messiah of the Deed, the healing Messiah. Read MATTHEW 8:1–11:1.

Find the Facts

What is Jesus doing in chapters 8 and 9? Where does this take place? What kinds of people does he encounter? How does he respond to them? To whom is the teaching in chapter 10 addressed? What kinds of issues are discussed?

1. *Overall, what seems most significant about the stories of Jesus as he goes about healing? With which story do you most identify? Why?*

2. *In chapter 10, what key phrases represent the main points of Jesus' instruction to the disciples?*

Matthew 8:1-17

MATTHEW 8:2-4 presents the first of a series of miracle stories in chapters 8–10 in which Matthew divides nine stories into groups of three and separates them with narrative or commentary. All of these activities take place in or near Capernaum and the Sea of Galilee.

A *miracle* can be defined as a phenomenon far exceeding the capacity of natural causes and attributed to the direct intervention of God. This definition is based on the scientific world view of the 18th and 19th centuries. The society of Jesus' day did not share this concept of nature based on immutable laws. Nor, it should be noted, do 20th-century scientists! In any case, New Testament miracle stories are not intended to challenge our scientific understandings; rather they point to God's power entering into the world through the incarnation of Jesus. The miracles demonstrate the benevolent saving nature of God's power. When the miracles are classified as either healing miracles or nature miracles, there are far more of the former.

Unlike miracle stories in other literature of the time, the gospel miracles never affect anyone adversely; in no instance is the power used for Jesus himself. In fact, the temptation to misuse power was the issue Jesus struggled with in the wilderness (4:1-11). For Matthew, showing Jesus as a miracle worker was an important piece of evidence that Jesus is the Messiah. The prototype miracle worker is Moses, through whom "signs and wonders" accomplish the deliverance of Israel from bondage. Likewise Jesus' miraculous acts in themselves are almost secondary to the deeper significance in the stories.

Lepers, for instance, were considered unclean and excluded from the community. Jesus frees the leper in 8:2-4 to rejoin the Jewish community according to the ritual commanded by Moses (LEV. 14:2ff). .◈

The story of the centurion (8:5-13), a Roman officer and not a Jew, demonstrates that Jesus responds to non-Jews, a reminder of the universality of Christ's mission. The centurion expresses a degree of faith that Jesus has not found among Jews. Jesus also responds to the needs of women, as in the healing of Peter's mother-in-law (8:14-15). In 8:16-17 Jesus heals people who are possessed with demons, spirits regarded as agents of illness. Matthew concludes with a typical rabbinical formula invoking Hebrew scripture to support his point that Jesus fulfills the law and the prophets.

3. *What elements do the stories of the leper and the centurion have in common? With what attitude do the two people approach Jesus? How does Jesus respond to each? What is significant about touching the leper and offering to go to the home of the centurion? Of what passages in the Sermon on the Mount do these actions remind you?*

4. *What are some characteristics of God's power as illustrated in these stories? For whose benefit does God display power? In what ways can we share God's power today? Who needs to be empowered in our society?*

Matthew 8:18—9:8

Verses 18-22 constitute an interlude in the cycle of miracle stories. Jesus is ready to move to another location, the other side of the Sea of Galilee, and pauses to comment on the demands of discipleship. Following Jesus will not be an easy life (8:20). A decision to follow him must take precedence over every other loyalty (8:22). The title *Son of man*, which Jesus often uses to describe himself, occurs here for the first time. Sometimes the title refers to the Son of man coming in glory at the end of the age, sometimes to Jesus' suffering and death, and sometimes (as here) to the powerful yet humble servant of the earthly ministry.

The next group of stories includes a nature miracle (Jesus calming the storm) and two more healing miracles. Verse 23 supplies the clue to the underlying significance of the boat story. Jesus gets into the boat; the disciples follow him, giving us further insight into the nature of discipleship. Following Jesus, as indicated in 8:18-22, may take us into stormy waters. Note that Jesus sleeps peacefully until the frightened disciples wake him up. Jesus demonstrates trust in God in the midst of turmoil.

In the next story (8:28-34) Jesus deals with two demoniacs who have been living in tombs, thought to be places of unclean spirits, and who are a constant menace to travelers. The evil spirits recognize Jesus and know that he will cast them out of the two men; they do not want to leave the area so they ask to enter into the swine. Jesus permits this, but then the swine drown themselves and, presumably, the demons as well. A conqueror of demons may also be a demon, so the people beg Jesus to leave.

Back in Capernaum, Jesus heals a paralytic (9:1-8). Again we find a level of greater significance than the miraculous healing itself. Though Jesus responds to the request for physical healing (9:6), he goes beyond to the heart of the matter. His deepest concern is for the patient's spiritual health. Remember that ancient Jewish thought considered illness to be the result of sin. Jesus' statement of forgiveness provokes a debate; the scribes accuse him of blasphemy, a foreshadowing of the official opposition that will bring him to the cross.

Consider:

5. According to 8:18-22, what are the costs of discipleship? Compare the story of the storm with 7:24-27. What do each of these passages say to you about how to approach times of difficulty?

6. Why do you think Jesus responds to the paralytic with two kinds of healing? List words that describe physical paralysis. What would it be like to be spiritually paralyzed? In what ways does forgiveness release us from such paralysis?

Matthew 9:9-17

This section of MATTHEW is the second interlude between groups of miracle stories. We learn a little more about the nature of discipleship from the events recounted here. Jesus calls a tax collector (9:9), again establishing a close relationship with one of society's outcasts. Tax collectors were unpopular both because of their collaboration with the Romans and because of their unjust demands. Sinners, perhaps having heard of his treatment of the paralytic, and more tax collectors promptly show up for dinner. The Pharisees object to Jesus' association with these classes of people, but Jesus explains that he is here to serve those who need him most. In verse 13, Jesus quotes HOSEA 6:6, one of many Old Testament texts in which prophets hammer home the message that God cares more for loving, merciful behavior than for "correct" religious practice.

Jesus then employs three images to respond to John's disciples who want to know why Jesus' disciples do not fast. Jesus explains through the image of the wedding celebration that fasting, a sign of mourning, is inappropriate at this time. Through the images of new and old clothes and new and old wine skins, Jesus suggests that the vitality of his way calls for new and joyous forms of expression.

Consider:

7. *What does verse 15 reveal about Jesus? about our life with Jesus?*

8. *Where in your life do you experience tension between old and new ways? between tradition and innovation? What do the images in 9:16-17 suggest about how to deal with this tension?*

Matthew 9:18-38

This passage includes the third trio of miracles; Jesus now ministers to the dead, the blind and the dumb. The healing of the ruler's daughter (9:18-26) further illustrates the life-giving newness Jesus talks about (9:16-17). The healing of the woman on the way to the ruler's house underscores the importance of the supplicant's faith in Jesus' saving power. Next Jesus heals two blind men after first questioning them about their faith. As with others Jesus has healed, faith in his power is the only precondition.

In the third episode Jesus heals a dumb man by casting out his demon. The twofold reaction to this miracle is significant. While the crowds marvel and spread the good news, the Pharisees make an ominous accusation that highlights the theme of opposition, building up as the gospel proceeds. Verses 35-36 provide another summary statement of Jesus' teaching, preaching and healing ministry. Expressing that the Lord has need of laborers, verses 37-38 set the scene for the second discourse—the missionary task—in chapter 10.

Consider:

9. In verses 18-24 there are three main characters besides Jesus. Describe how each encounters Jesus. Do you identify more with the ruler, the ruler's daughter or the woman who touches Jesus' garment? How does this identification help you to understand the nature of your own faith?

10. What is the tension between spreading the good news and the opposition this engenders? Where do you see this tension in today's society?

Matthew 10:1-23

In chapter 10 Jesus gathers the twelve individuals he has called to begin the compassionate work of "shepherds" (9:36-37). He shares his authority with them (10:1) and, beginning with 10:5, instructs them regarding their mission. The number twelve suggests the twelve tribes of Israel. Gathering all Israel into the kingdom is the initial task of the twelve disciples (10:6). MATTHEW 10:7 summarizes their primary message: God's kingdom is available here and now (3:2; 4:17).

The disciples are to mirror the actions of Jesus as described in chapters 8–9 (10:8). Like Jesus they are to work without pay, travel light and trust local hospitality (10:9-10). "Worthy" (10:11) simply means likely to be open to the message of the kingdom. If the message of peace is rejected, the disciple should not waste more time in that place, but move on, leaving judgment to God (7:1). Sodom and Gomorrah were understood to be examples of extreme wickedness (EZEK. 16:49-50).

Consider:

11. *List some of the elements of the task of discipleship discussed in 10:1-15. What personal qualities would equip an individual to undertake this task? Compare your list to 5:3-11.*

Read Luke 9 + 10 ¹⁻⁶   Mark is parallel

memorize 12 apostles
① Simon Peter
② Andrew
③ James, son of Zebedee
④ John
⑤ Philip
⑥ Bartholomew (Nathaniel)
⑦ Thomas

⑧ Matthew (Levi) tax collector
⑨ James son of Alphaeus
⑩ Thaddaeus (father of James the f.) also Jude
⑪ Simon Zealot
⑫ Judas Iscariot - son g

Isaiah 61
Sodom & Gomorrah

Matthew 10:16–11:1

Just as the missionary disciples share Jesus' mission and ministry, so will they share his persecution and martyrdom. They are like defenseless sheep among hostile wolves. Serpents represent the idea of cleverness and shrewdness; innocent means purity of intention, clarity of purpose; in rabbinical literature the dove often symbolizes Israel—patient, submissive and faithful.

Verse 21 interjects an apocalyptic note. Division among families was understood to be a sign of end times. To "endure" (10:22) means to suffer patiently, and "the end" could refer to the end of the persecution, the end of the individual's life or the end of the age. MATTHEW 10:24-25 reiterates the idea that the disciples will share in the fate of their master; rejection and persecution are inevitable.

Jesus speaks words of comfort and reassurance in verses 26-33. Jesus' message is not a secret, but intended to be shouted from the housetop (the traditional place from which public announcements were made). The disciples may do this without fear since God's own loving power stands with each of them.

Verses 34-39 spell out the high cost of commitment. Disciples must be prepared for conflict (10:34), family strife, and be ready, if necessary, to choose Jesus over the closest personal ties. Verses 35-36 refer to MICAH 7:6 in which the prophet warns of judgment against the corruptions and pretensions of Jerusalem.

In verse 39, "to lose one's life" could mean to die a violent death, or it could picture the difficulty of self-denial. To "find" one's life means to obtain, win or preserve life. True life is found through Jesus.

The conclusion of the discourse (10:40-42) returns to the theme of hospitality and expresses an idea familiar to Judaism, that a person's emissary or agent is like the person himself. Here is a corollary to the previously stated principle that the disciples share the fate of the Master. Those who receive the disciples, receive Jesus. MATTHEW 11:1 is the concluding formula for this discourse.

12. *In your opinion, how broadly are the first-century missionary instructions to be applied? What general principles do they suggest for the Church today? for your own life?*

13. *What do you think of the concept that an emissary is virtually identical to the person who sends the emissary? Who do you think performs this kind of representative function for Jesus today? Do you ever think of yourself in this role? Why or why not?*

Group Activities

1. The first missionary journey for the disciples was to areas close to home, to people like themselves.

   Divide into groups of three or four and distribute paper and pencils. Ask groups to imagine that they are a team about to evangelize their community. Each group is to write a set of instructions for the project. Suggest that they review MATTHEW 10:5-39 and note general principles; then write instructions in today's idiom, using contemporary illustrations.

   Allow groups about 15 minutes to work, before inviting them to share their work with the whole group.

2. List on newsprint, whiteboard or chalkboard the nine miracle stories in MATTHEW 8–10, in any order that group members recall. Divide into groups of three or four. Ask each group to pick one of the nine accounts and to make up a story of what happened next, focusing on the healed person's quality of life. Suggest that they imagine as many details as possible, for example: What family members and friends were involved? Whose lives were changed and in what ways? What did they learn about God? about Jesus? about their relationship to God?

   Invite groups to act out or tell their stories to the others. Note: If the group is small this could be done individually or in pairs.

3. Distribute newspapers, magazines, scissors, glue and large sheets of newsprint. Working in pairs, look for illustrations (pictures or stories) of the kinds of people Jesus heals. Share the collages and discuss:
   - In what ways are the needs of the outcasts—or people with diminished rights—being met in today's society?
   - Who is ministering to them most effectively?
   - What role is played, or should be played, by the Church and Christian individuals?

Journal Meditation

The miracle stories show Jesus relating to individuals, identifying their specific needs and releasing them from pain, estrangement, fear, confusion or even death itself. Each individual thus healed sees another facet of Jesus' ability to heal and restore. In what areas of your life would you like to experience Jesus' healing and restoration? Approach Jesus and ask for his help. How does knowing Emmanuel (God with us) help you to take a first step toward healing?

Stepstone To Prayer

Lord, help me to risk losing the obvious that I might gain the mystery of life lived with you.

Matthew 11:2–12:50
Opposition and Response

IN CHAPTERS 11 AND 12, Jesus responds to questioners who express doubts and challenge his authority. These disputes increase throughout Matthew's gospel, eventually culminating in open conflict and death. Read MATTHEW 11–12.

Find The Facts

What disturbs Jesus about the response of many to his ministry thus far? Who are Jesus' questioners? What do they want to know? Of what crimes do the Pharisees accuse Jesus? What request does Jesus refuse?

Consider:

1. What overall themes can you identify in this section?

2. What forms of opposition does Jesus encounter? How does he respond to them?

3. What do you think is the basic point of disagreement between Jesus and the Pharisees?

Matthew 11:2-15

Jesus' ministry has raised many questions for his contemporaries, questions that Matthew knew were also being asked by the Church of the late first century. We ask similar questions today: Who is Jesus? How are we to respond to him?

John the Baptist, now in prison, is one of the people who ask about Jesus' identity. News about Jesus raises a basic question for him: Is Jesus the One? (11:3). John expected a different kind of Messiah. John looked for a judge (MT. 3:11-12). Jesus says he has not come to destroy, but to heal, restore and save.

Jesus replies to John's messengers by describing his actions. His words are reminiscent of ISAIAH 35:5-6, a passage describing Yahweh's salvation of Israel. The actions of Jesus, then, are evidence that the messianic age announced by the prophets has arrived.

Jesus then speaks to the crowds. He acknowledges that they correctly identify John the Baptist as a prophet (11:7-10). In fact, says Jesus, John is the greatest of all who stand in the old tradition; yet even the least of the disciples of Jesus are greater than any prophet for they have entered God's kingdom (11:11), available to all who receive Jesus' message.

4. *In Matthew 11:3, John the Baptist poses the central question of Matthew's gospel: Is Jesus the Messiah? Restate Jesus' answer in your own words. Why would John have recognized this as an affirmative reply? To whom is this question important today?*

5. *Read Matthew 11:4, 15. To what does Jesus appeal to convince people of his authenticity? By using our own eyes and ears what can we "see" and "hear" about Jesus in this passage? in our daily lives?*

Matthew 11:16-30

Jesus now expresses his frustration with the lack of response to his ministry in certain cities. It seems impossible to satisfy his contemporaries. They respond neither to Jesus' joy (piping) or John's asceticism (wailing). Nonetheless, the deeds of Jesus and his followers—preaching, teaching and healing—will speak for themselves.

Jesus voices a lament over the cities that ignored his healing miracles and turned a deaf ear to the kingdom proclamation. "Cities," as distinguished from the people in general, refer to organized communities, perhaps to the leaders of such cities. Jesus unfavorably compares these cities to several unrepentant cities of the Old Testament. The Gentile cities of Tyre and Sidon were punished for their pride. Sodom was synonymous with injustice and oppression.

Jesus turns to prayer and praises God when faced with this lack of response. As he prays (vv. 25-26) he shares a significant insight; it will not be those who are well-trained in the law who will respond to his work, but "babes," the poor in spirit, the hungry ones, the seekers.

Verse 27 describes Jesus' relationship with God, and 28-30 invite others to share it. Those who are heavy laden might be the ones scorned by the Pharisees for their inability to obey the law in all its detailed complexity. Rabbis used "yoke" as a symbol for the Mosaic law; Jesus' yoke will be different. Instead of a heavy burden of rules and regulations, Jesus' followers will imitate his gentleness and humility.

6. With whom today do you think Jesus feels frustrated? Who are today's open and responsive spiritual "babes"? How are they reached by Jesus' call?

7. What heavy burden would you like to exchange for the light yoke of Jesus? What rest does Jesus promise? Describe what that rest might feel like.

Matthew 12:1-21

Start with 12:13

This section recounts the first of three challenges from the Pharisees. We have already been introduced to their practice of watching Jesus, we have seen them try to trap him with a wrong answer or catch him engaged in forbidden actions. Some of the Pharisees focus obsessively on the law, centering their religion in observance of the law and its severe interpretation. They had, for instance, identified thirty-nine types of work prohibited on the sabbath. Rubbing grain (12:1) counted as preparation of food, one of the prohibitions. Jesus counters with an appeal to David, who ate holy food when he was in need (1 SAM. 21:1-6), and to the priests who minister in the sanctuary on the sabbath (12:3-5). Besides citing these precedents to defend his actions, Jesus suggests that the basic principle involved is more important than a specific application (12:6-8).

Observance of the sabbath, the seventh day in the Jewish week, developed along with the religion of the synagogue. Like synagogue worship, sabbath observance did not depend on the temple and could be practiced everywhere. In fact, observing sabbath traditions identified Jews and distinguished them from Gentiles. Verses 9-14 find Jesus again offending the Pharisees with unlawful sabbath activity. This time he defends himself more strongly, stating that there is no time when it is prohibited to do good. As usual, Jesus stresses the spirit of the law over the letter of the law.

We know that Jesus observed the sabbath and occasionally taught in the synagogues (MK. 6:2; LK. 4:16, 31). But he wants to go beyond surface legalism to the basic concept of sabbath observance: The sabbath exists for human welfare (MK. 2:27). Jesus fails to convince the Pharisees, however, who plot ways in which to destroy him (12:14). Meanwhile, Jesus quietly withdraws, continuing his healing ministry. Matthew quotes from Isaiah again to show Jesus as a meek but powerful servant, whose ministry, though ignored and opposed by many, will broaden to include all peoples (12:18-21).

8. Where have you heard Jesus speak against excessive legalism before? (See Mt. 7:1, 9:13.) What passages from the Sermon on the Mount illuminate Jesus' statement that "something greater than the temple" is involved in sabbath observance? (See Mt. 5:23; 7:21.)

9. How do you view your own sabbath (Sunday) observance? Are there things you do differently on that day of the week? Why? Read Mark 2:27-28. What difference does it make that the sabbath was made for people? that the sabbath was made for you? that Jesus is the Lord of the sabbath?

Matthew 12:22-37

The healing of the demoniac in verse 22 offers a concrete example of what Jesus is doing in 12:15. This healing provokes sharply divided reactions. At issue is the source of Jesus' power. The crowd, amazed, speculates that this might be the Son of David, a messianic title popular in Judaism from the middle of the first century. But the Pharisees say Jesus' power over demons comes from his being in the service of Beelzebul, that is, Satan. This was equivalent to accusing Jesus of magic, a capital offense.

Jesus counters the accusation with a series of illustrations and warnings. First, he points out that any organization that fights against itself will be destroyed. This would be the case if Satan cast out Satan. But if God casts out Satan, then God's kingdom is really here (12:25-28). Besides, Pharisees also cast out demons (12:27); are they too in service to Beelzebul?

Neutrality in regard to Jesus is impossible (11:28). The "unforgivable sin" is the sin of calling good evil and attributing the work of God's Holy Spirit to the evil spirit (11:31-32).

Jesus issues another warning through the image of trees and their fruits 12:33-37). Good fruit comes from good trees; bad trees produce bad fruit. Similarly, the malicious words of the Pharisees reveal evil hearts. The internal condition of a person determines the quality of the person's words and deeds (12:33-35). Verses 36-37 summarize Jesus' point: words reveal character and we are held accountable for them.

10. How do you explain the radically different responses to Jesus' power? Which of Jesus' illustrations help you to understand the nature of this power? Why?

11. To what extent do you agree with verse 30? In what sense is neutrality about Jesus an impossibility?

Matthew 12:38-50

The scribes and Pharisees request a sign from Jesus. "Sign" is not synonymous with miracle, but carries more the sense of proof or evidence. The Old Testament abounds with "signs" showing that Yahweh is present and active, for example, in the ten plagues sent to Egypt (Ex. 3:20). Jesus' challengers want a convincing display of supernatural power that authenticates his authority. Jesus is impatient with the request and calls the scribes and Pharisees "adulterous," unfaithful to God. Therefore they shall receive but one sign, the death of the Son of man. The symbolic significance of the Jonah story is twofold: First, Jesus' rebirth will follow his death, as Jonah's freedom followed his captivity in the large fish. Second, Jesus' followers have an obligation to bring the knowledge of God to all nations, not just to Israel, as God commanded Jonah to preach to the non-Jewish Ninevites. The irony increases as Jesus points out that the pagan Ninevites repented (Jon. 3:5) and Sheba ("queen of the South") came to hear the wisdom of Solomon (1 Kg. 10:1-13). Yet the current "evil generation" of Israelites is rejecting someone even greater than Solomon (12:38-42).

Verses 43-45 constitute another warning. Though the unclean spirit (demon) has been cast out, something needs to take it's place. If a person does not fill the space with something holy, the emptiness will invite occupation; more devils will come than were there in the first place.

In MATTHEW 12:46-50, Jesus turns from his blood family ties and declares his true family to be his disciples, those who have chosen to follow him in doing God's will. Jesus thus ends this section affirming that, though many reject him, many also accept him and form relationships with him, relationships as intimate as those of family members.

12. In what sense are Jesus' remarks about unclean spirits (12:43-45) relevant to our generation? What are some of the things that cause trouble in our lives today? unhealthy habits? cynical attitudes? To what extent is it wise advice to replace these "demons" with more constructive behaviors or ways of thinking?

13. What is Jesus saying about his family in verses 47-50? To whom will Jesus relate in intimate family fashion? What is his relationship to you?

Group Activities

1. Divide into three groups. Ask each group to prepare a contemporary newscaster's report of the disputes between Jesus and the Pharisees. Invite Group 1 to cover MATTHEW 12:1-8, Group 2, MATTHEW 12:9-15 and Group 3, MATTHEW 12:22-29. Suggest that each group choose a reporter from among its group members.

   When groups are ready, reassemble the larger group and ask reporters to present their newscast.

2. Distribute Bibles. Ask volunteers to read DEUTERONOMY 12-15, EXODUS 23:12 and MARK 2:27. Discuss:
   • What is the purpose of the day of rest? How closely does this purpose relate to Jesus' statement in MARK 2:27?
   • What is the relationship between the original concept of keeping a holy sabbath and the legalistic approach advocated by the Pharisees of Jesus' time?

   Ask volunteers to share childhood memories of what their families did or did not do on Sundays. Discuss:
   • Which of these were meaningful? Why?
   • Which were trivial or got in the way of the purpose of sabbath observance?

   Brainstorm sensible guidelines for making Sunday a time of rest and refreshment. List ideas on newsprint, whiteboard or chalkboard.

3. Distribute paper and crayons or colored felt markers. Ask group members to draw pictures or symbol that illustrate MATTHEW 11:28-30. Pair off and share pictures and symbols with partners. Ask pairs to discuss:
   • What is Jesus' yoke like for you?
   • What is Jesus' rest like for you?

   After pairs have finished their discussions, reassemble the group and invite group members to compose prayers based on their discussions.

   End by inviting volunteers to pray their prayers aloud.

Journal Meditation

In MATTHEW 11–12, several people raise questions about Jesus. What questions do you have about Jesus' power and authority? How do you think Jesus would respond to your questions? Write an imaginary dialogue between you and Jesus.

Stepstone To Prayer

Lord Jesus, your yoke is easy and your burden is light. Help me to...

Matthew 13:1-52
Seeing and Hearing the Messiah

AFTER THE NARRATIVE ACTION of chapters 11 and 12, we pause to reflect on MATTHEW 13, another significant body of teaching. Jesus teaches in parables, telling story after story to illustrate the nature of God's kingdom. Read MATTHEW 13.

Find The Facts

To whom does Jesus direct his teaching? What teaching technique does he use? How many parables are in this chapter? What are some recurring images? What reactions to his teaching does Jesus encounter? Which verse marks the end of the discourse?

Consider:

1. Review Matthew 11-12. What is the context for the teaching found in Matthew 13?

2. What do you think is the main theme of the parables in Matthew 13? Underline a verse that seems to summarize Jesus' main point.

Matthew 13:1-23

Verses 1-3 set the scene for the third discourse. Jesus comes out of the house and sits down, an indication that he is going to teach. So many people gather that he climbs into a boat to address them, making certain that everyone will hear, choosing a mode of teaching familiar to his audience.

Jesus has already used several different methods to convey his message of the present reality of God's kingdom: preaching and healing (4:23); explaining that the kingdom represents messianic fulfillment (5:17-20); healing specific categories of illness (chap. 8); and answering his opponents (chap. 12). Now he chooses to speak in parables. Parables may sound somewhat mysterious, like secret codes that can be cracked only by a few insiders, but according to this gospel Jesus intends the opposite. As he explains in 13:13, his concern is that even though people have seen his deeds and heard his teaching many still do not understand. The disciples have heard and accepted Jesus' message, and their faith opens them to even deeper understanding (13:11). The parables will offer an opportunity for others to enter into this kind of faith dialogue.

The parable, a favorite device of Jewish teachers, may be a story, a brief metaphor or a proverb designed to illustrate a single point of teaching. Jesus' parables rely on the commonplace experience of the hearers, inviting them to make a judgment on an ordinary situation, then transfer it to a spiritual setting. Though the stories may lend themselves to allegorical interpretation (13:18-23 and 37-43 may be interpretations by the early Church), searching for point-by-point meaning in the details usually obscures the main point.

In MATTHEW 13 we find seven parables plus some private interpretation for the disciples. In the parable of the sower, the sower "went out to sow" much as Jesus "went out" to teach. (Compare 13:1 and 13:4.) Palestinian farmers of Jesus' day sowed their seed before plowing the field. Casting seed everywhere wastes a lot of seed but ensures an abundant harvest. The situation is similar to that of Jesus, who continues to broadcast God's message even in the face of opposition from officials and lack of response from the people.

3. Another name for the parable of the sower could be "the parable of the different kinds of soil." What kinds of soil are mentioned in 13:4-8? How do they suggest different kinds of human response? How can we cultivate our own soil so that the seed of God's word can grow in us?

4. Underline the references to seeing and hearing in Matthew 13:9-17. How does verse 9 help you to understand Jesus' point in verses 11-13? In what ways is faith itself a help in deepening our understanding of Jesus?

5. How is it possible to see and hear the truth without being able to understand it? What things in our lives prevent us from hearing God's word in meaningful ways? Which ones cause you the most trouble? What can you do about it?

Matthew 13:24-30 and 36-43

Continuing with the images of sower, seed, growth and harvest, the second parable compares the kingdom of heaven to the situation of a man who sowed good seed. A second sower (an enemy!) sows weeds in the same field so that the growing plants are all mixed up together. The servants are distressed but the householder is content to let them grow together. At the time of harvest the situation will be resolved. The weeds, originally sown to inhibit the growth of the wheat, will be burned, their intention unfulfilled. Life in our world is a mixture of good and bad, but Jesus expresses confidence that God's goodness will prevail in the end.

Verses 36-43 offer an allegorical interpretation of Jesus' parable, possibly the work of the gospel writer. In this interpretation, the Son of man represents the risen Christ, the field represents the world, the good seed represent the true disciples, and the weeds represent those who do evil or cause others to do evil. Harvest time is often an image for the last judgment in both the Old Testament and the New Testament. The interpretation ends like the first parable, with a challenge to hear and understand. Those who hear will experience the kingdom.

Consider:

6. *What do you think of the householder's decision not to weed the field? What threatens our growth as Christians in today's world? What helps us to grow in the midst of pressure?*

7. What are some characteristics of weeds? of wheat? What are the weeds and wheat in you life with others? in your inner life?

Matthew 13:31-35

These two short parables give us further insight into the nature of God's kingdom. MATTHEW 13:4-9 identified the kingdom with spreading the word; verses 24-30 indicated that the kingdom grows even in the presence of evil; verses 31-33 now show that the kingdom grows to greatness from tiny beginnings.

The mustard seed is a proverbial example of smallness. Actually, mustard seeds grow into bushes, not trees. MATTHEW 13:32 connects the image of protective branches with an Old Testament metaphor for Israel in the messianic age (EZEK. 17:22-24). Jesus, who himself deals with life on a small scale in the villages and with individuals, may be suggesting that we do not need to import an impressive tree from elsewhere in order to further God's kingdom.

The second parable also points out the amazing contrast between small, unpromising beginnings and the grand result. Here another well-known symbol (yeast symbolized evil and corruption) is used in a different way. The clever woman hides a tiny lump of the unprepossessing substance in a ridiculously large amount of flour, and it is sufficient.

According to verses 31-32, the kingdom of heaven is like a mustard seed sowed by a man or a lump of leaven used by a woman. These parables suggest that God can create wonderful things from inauspicious beginnings. How tiny and insignificant seem the tiny seed or the dried yeast. How powerful their effect!

Verses 34-35 conclude the portion of Jesus' teaching that is addressed to the crowds. The interpretation in 36-43 and, apparently, the three parables that follow are addressed to the disciples alone. The prophet referred to in verse 35 is Asaph the seer (2 CHR. 29:30) and the quotation is from PSALM 78. As in verse 13, Matthew emphasizes that Jesus speaks in parables, not to mystify, but to reveal what has previously been hidden.

Consider:

8. *What must be done with the seed and the leaven before growth takes place? What significance do you see in God's desire to work through human agents? What small seed have you planted recently for which you have high hopes? How will its growth further God's kingdom?*

9. What things, previously hidden, do these two parables reveal to you? How do the images of seeds and leaven help you to see and hear Jesus more clearly?

Matthew 13:44-52

The parables of verses 44 and 45 emphasize the value of the kingdom and the joyful response of those who discover it. The treasure of the kingdom is worth any price. Both treasure and pearls are symbols for wisdom in the Old Testament (Pr. 21:20; Job 28:18). Here they represent a new form of wisdom.

In the first situation an ordinary laborer plowing someone else's field accidentally comes across buried treasure. Surprised and delighted he realizes instantly that possessing this treasure will change his whole life. It is worth everything to buy that field, and he takes immediate action.

The merchant stands in contrast to the poor laborer, but they share something in common. A wealthy connoisseur of fine jewels, the merchant deliberately seeks to build up his collection. But when he finds one gem that surpasses all others in value, he too responds with total commitment. Both the laborer and the merchant find the treasure in the ordinary course of their lives. God's kingdom is available to rich and poor alike, to anyone who "sees," "hears" and responds.

The last of the parables in chapter 13 features the image of a dragnet pulled by two boats collecting everything in its path. Like the parable of the wheat and the weeds, it indicates a mixture of good and bad and concludes with the certainty that in the end evil will be rejected and punished.

In the conclusion to this section (13:51-52), the disciples say that they understand the message of the kingdom. Jesus then addresses them again in parabolic language. Scribes (those trained in the law) are those who, like a householder whose treasury contains both what is new and what is old, will be able to understand the new message as a fulfillment of the traditional law (5:17). Many have thought this passage to be the gospel writer's self-portrait.

Verse 53 is Matthew's usual formula for ending a discourse. Jesus concludes his teaching and prepares to move elsewhere.

Consider:

10. *Are you more like the laborer or the merchant? Are you more likely to discover an important truth by accident or to uncover it by careful searching? What do you do when you find such treasures? In what way is God's kingdom a treasure to you?*

11. *Write a summary of what God's kingdom is like based on Matthew 13. Which of the parables speaks to you most deeply? Why?*

Group Activities

1. Divide into two groups. Give each group newsprint and markers.

   Ask Group 1 to brainstorm and record:
   - What have been the mustard seeds for our community? Where have tiny beginnings made an impact or grown into something impressive?

   Ask Group 2 to brainstorm and record:
   - What has been the leaven in our community? What unimportant or unappealing people or things or ideas have been agents of transformation for us?

   Come back together and share your findings. What evidence do you see of fruitful results from small beginnings? How do such stories encourage us when we feel small and insignificant?

2. List on newsprint, whiteboard or chalkboard as many images as group members can recall from the parables in chapter 13. That the images in the parables are primarily agricultural is not surprising; Jesus lived and worked among people in an agricultural economy. Working in pairs, discuss:
   - What are some images of the agents of change in our contemporary setting? (for example, the corporation, an educational institution, an industrial town, the world of computers, etc.)
   - Select an image and consider the changes brought about by it. Compose a modern parable that begins, "The kingdom of God is like..."

   Invite pairs to tell their parables to the group.

3. Pass out paper and colored crayons, felt markers or finger paints. Ask each person to select one of the parables or a particular image from a parable and to illustrate how it enables us to see God's kingdom or to hear Jesus' message more clearly.

   In groups of three or four, share the pictures and explain them if you would like to.

   Reassemble the group and ask volunteers to share new insights from the small-group sharing.

Journal Meditation

Reflect on the parable of the woman who hid the leaven and the man who found hidden treasure. What things are hidden deep within yourself that represent precious treasure? What within yourself is like leaven with the capacity to transform your whole being? Describe the treasure or the leaven or draw a picture of it. How does this treasure or leaven enrich your understanding of Emmanuel (God with us)?

Stepstone To Prayer

God, help me to more fully understand the nature of your kingdom.

Matthew 13:53–16:20
The Messiah Revealed

JESUS NOW EXPANDS HIS ITINERANT MINISTRY against a background of growing hostility from authorities and rejection by the people; it concludes with Peter's recognition of Jesus as "the Christ, Son of the Living God," the literary climax and turning point of this gospel. After 16:20, everything points toward Jerusalem. Read MATTHEW 13:54–16:20.

Find the Facts

In what kinds of activities is Jesus engaged? Where do the events take place? What happens to John the Baptist? With whom does Jesus debate? About what does Jesus warn the disciples? Who correctly identifies Jesus?

Consider:

1. What familiar themes do you find in this section? Underline passages that remind you of ideas developed in chapters 1-13.

2. Who are some of the people who reject Jesus in this section? Which story of hostility to Jesus strikes you as most ominous? Why?

3. With which character in Matthew 13:53–16:20 do you feel the strongest identification? Why?

Matthew 13:53—14:12

The last portion of chapter 13 and the first two verses of 14 are both stories of rejection and misunderstanding. Jesus returns to the neighborhood where he grew up and, like a good Jewish rabbi, he teaches in the synagogue. Once again he encounters suspicion and rejection. The people see him as a member of a perfectly ordinary family and are unable to hear and respond to his message (13:53-58). Immediately (14:1-2) Matthew recounts another story of misunderstanding. Herod, who is Herod Antipas, the son of Herod the Great (who tried to murder the infant Jesus, MT. 2:16-18) and Tetrarch of Galilee and Perea, speculates that Jesus must be the resurrected John the Baptist. Perhaps he feels some guilt around this issue since the ensuing story indicates beheading John the Baptist was not Herod's idea (14:9), though Herod wished him dead (14:5). Or he may fear the political consequences since it was illegal under Jewish law to execute a person without trial.

The double rejection, first by friends and neighbors, then by the political leadership, recalls 11:16-19, where Jesus laments the difficulty of pleasing the present generation. In an additional irony, Herod's mistaken identification attributes Jesus' power to John the Baptist, who, though a great prophet, struggled to understand Jesus (11:11).

Consider:

4. *Why do you think Jesus' neighbors reject him? Why is it sometimes difficult to recognize Jesus in the ordinary areas of life?*

5. *What do you think caused Herod to come to a false conclusion about Jesus? In what ways do political concerns, family relationships and customs of society prevent people from understanding Jesus' message today? What barriers to understanding exist in your own life?*

Matthew 14:13-36

Jesus withdraws upon receiving the news of John the Baptist's death, a reaction similar to his response to hearing of John's imprisonment (4:12). As in the earlier incident, John's fate seems to signal a new phase for Jesus' ministry. Many of the stories that follow will employ images of bread, feeding or eating, an image of great significance to the early Church.

The feeding of the crowds is a story repeated six times in the gospels (MK. 6:30-44; LK. 9:10-17; JN. 6:1-13; MT 15:32-9; MK. 8:1-10) and one rich with symbolic meanings for Christians. The story begins with compassion and healing and ends with an unexpectedly satisfying meal on the hillside. The episode evokes a number of biblical images: Moses feeding the people with manna (Ex. 16), Elisha multiplying food for the hungry (2 KG. 4:42-44), and the messianic kingdom represented as a lavish feast (Is. 25:6). The account stands in sharp contrast to the preceding story of another meal, the sinister and gory birthday feast in Herod's palace. Jesus' simple meal (loaves and dried fish were the common diet of the poor) brings peace and satisfaction to all who partake.

The Eucharistic overtones are obvious: Jesus takes the bread, blesses God for the bread, breaks the bread and gives it to all. The people are satisfied and the crumbs are carefully gathered up.

The next story, another nature miracle, recalls 8:23-27. Again we see Jesus at ease with nature, this time walking on the sea. Some interpret this story as an allegory of the Church (the boat) buffeted on all sides by evil (darkness and waves), yet saved by her Lord. Verse 26 is a third example of misunderstanding. The disciples who are now Jesus' true family (12:49) do not recognize him in the dark. Like Herod, they leap to a wrong conclusion based on their fears. After things settle down (vv. 32-33), they acknowledge him as the Son of God, a true, but as yet incomplete identification (16:15).

Perhaps many of us will identify with the impetuous Peter who, even in his eagerness to accept what Jesus offers, loses heart and flounders. Peter's doubt stands in his way. Jesus reaches out with a steady hand of rescue. With the boat safely landed, Jesus continues healing the sick, many of whom have such strong faith that they desire only to touch the fringe of his garment. When people reach out in faith, Jesus meets their needs.

Consider

6. *What is the disciples' role in the feeding of the five thousand? What do you think Jesus is trying to teach them by encouraging them to participate in his ministry? What kinds of help does Jesus' body, the Church, need today in the task of "feeding" the multitudes? What is your place in this task?*

7. *What prevented Peter from reaching Jesus over the water? What fears keep you from recognizing Christ in your life? What fears keep you from reaching him when you try?*

Matthew 15:1-20

The ongoing dispute between Jesus and the Pharisees accelerates with the arrival of a formal delegation from Jerusalem. These Pharisees and scribes make a serious charge, saying that Jesus' disciples violate the tradition of the elders (the body of interpretation that developed around the written law and was transmitted orally by rabbis over generations). Specifically, the disciples do not wash their hands before eating. This hand washing was not a matter of hygiene, but a ritual act to cleanse one from any accidental contact with objects considered ritually unclean. This was an important point to Pharisees, who were committed to maintaining Israel's separation from the unclean Gentiles. Jesus counters their charge with another, cleverly turning their own words against them. Pharisees, in their zeal for the tradition, have transgressed the most fundamental law, God's own commandment. For example, they allow people to reserve money for the temple instead of using it to care for their parents. The quotation from Isaiah (Is. 29:13) characterizes the Pharisees as hypocrites.

In verse 10 Jesus turns to the people and discusses ritual purity. He explains that what one eats is not what defiles. The Pharisees have been overly concerned about the wrong issue. The issue, as Jesus sees it, is not ritual defilement, but moral defilement. What comes from the heart is what matters to God. It is useless to worry about whether one is fit for ritual worship if one is not in proper relationship with other people. Verse 19, a call to focus on basic human problems, summarizes the Ten Commandments. Though this dispute deals with a controversy in the early Church, it may well challenge us to consider whether our own cherished traditions help or hinder us as we live out our faith.

Consider:

8. Which of your religious traditions belong to a written "law"? Which are based on "oral tradition" (that is, customs passed on from one generation to the next)? Why do some seem more essential than others? Which are most helpful to you as you try to avoid the kind of defilement Jesus talks about?

9. What is your definition of hypocrisy? Compare it to Isaiah's definition (15:8-9). Why does Jesus condemn the Pharisees for teaching human precepts as doctrines? How does this constitute hypocrisy? What is a more honest approach to sharing our beliefs with others?

Matthew 15:21-39

Here is a healing miracle with a new twist. Jesus ignores, then refuses a petitioner! Right after he has criticized the Pharisees for their separatist practices he seems to fall into the same trap, stating at first that his mission is only to the Jews. The Canaanite woman turns the tables in a remarkable way; she employs Jesus' own method of dispute, accepting his harsh metaphor (v. 26) with grace and wit, then turning it to her own advantage (v. 27). Jesus demonstrates his openness as he accepts her argument, commends her faith, and fulfills her request. Jesus stretches his understanding of his mission and responds to true belief.

The story is rich with images and ironies. The unclean Gentile woman addresses Jesus as Lord soon after the ritually-pure Pharisees attack him. The telling metaphor centers on bread as does the feeding of the five thousand, and the woman's willingness to eat only the crumbs poignantly recalls the twelve baskets full of crumbs left over from the hillside feast. In God's kingdom there is enough for all, even for those classified as outsiders.

In verse 29 Jesus goes up on a mountain and sits down, recalling the setting for the Sermon on the Mount (5:1). Matthew then summarizes the whole Galilean ministry in language reminiscent of ISAIAH 29:18-19 and 35:5-6. Great things have indeed come to pass. Moreover, these crowds are not only healed, but also fed. The early Church saw in the feeding miracles the prototype of their Eucharistic celebrations, hence the repetition of 14:14-21.

10. Why do you think Jesus changes his mind about healing the Canaanite woman? Was it her persistence? her argument? her faith? the fact that she, a Gentile, identified him as the Jewish Messiah? In what ways do you approach God with your needs and desires?

11. What connections do you see between the healing of the crowds and the feeding of the crowds? Look carefully at the sequence of events: The people came; Jesus healed them; they glorified God; Jesus fed them. What clues for your own journey do you find in this sequence?

Matthew 16:1-12

Once again officials seek out Jesus. Pharisees and Sadducees band together to demand a sign. Jesus replies much as he did on the previous occasion (12:38ff). They will not get the kind of sign they demand. Instead they will receive the sign of Jonah (12:39-40).

In 5-12 Jesus warns the disciples against the Pharisees and Sadducees, again using the bread imagery that has predominated in this section. The disciples still need to work on their understanding of Jesus; here (v. 7) they interpret his warning words literally (v. 6), thinking he is worried that they brought no bread. Jesus patiently reminds them of the significance of the "bread" he offers, and finally they understand that he likens the narrow teaching of the Pharisees and Sadducees to leaven, which, though it may not look significant, has great power. (See 13:33.)

Consider:

12. What were the signs of the times that Jesus says the Pharisees and Sadducees cannot interpret? What helps you to recognize God's activity in the world today?

Matthew 16:13-20

After many stories of belief and unbelief, recognition and mistaken identification, response and rejection, we come to a story that pulls together belief, recognition and response with one dramatic question and answer.

In verse 13 Jesus himself brings up the question of his identity. "Who do people say I am?" he asks the disciples. "Son of man" here is equivalent to "I." The answers are disappointing; speculation centers around heroes of the past. So Jesus presses on. But you, who do you say that I am? The impetuous Peter puts it all together. Jesus is the Christ (Messiah) and Son of the living God.

Jesus' responds with a blessing and a new name. Again, Old Testament images abound. For example, Jacob receives a blessing and a new name (Israel) in GENESIS 32:22-31. Blessing is also associated with covenant. God changes Abram's name to Abraham (GEN. 17:4-5) and promises fruitfulness; Jesus changes Simon's name to Peter and establishes the Church, which will also be fruitful and multiply through all nations. Bar-Jona probably identifies Simon as Son of John. The name Peter means rock. Jesus' body, the Church, will rest on this solid foundation. (See 7:24-25.) The rock is not Peter's stability of character, but his openness to revelation (v. 17) and the strength of his faith. With the new name or title comes new power and authority. As representative of the earthly Church, Peter's decisions will be ratified by God at the last judgment. Verses 18-19 (found only in MATTHEW) form the basis for the tradition of apostolic succession, and the Roman Catholic doctrine that Peter was the first of the bishops of Rome, head of the Church universal.

The time has not yet come to announce Jesus' full identity to others (v. 20). Jesus must first teach the disciples the full meaning of messiahship. Peter's confession thus marks a turning point in this gospel. The disciples now know who Jesus is and, beginning with verse 21, he begins to prepare them for the events in Jerusalem.

Consider:

13. *Why did people think Jesus was John the Baptist, Elijah or Jeremiah? In what ways does Peter's confession clarify the issue of Jesus' identity? How would you answer the same question today?*

14. *How do you interpret the insight, power and authority given to Peter? In what ways do these continue in today's Church? As a member of Christ's body, how do you share this insight, power and authority?*

Group Activities

1. As a group, list on chalkboard or newsprint the places in MATTHEW 13:53–16:12 in which reference is made to Jesus' identity, for example, 13:57 (prophet) and 14:2 (John the Baptist). Divide into small groups and assign one of the references to each. Let the small groups discuss:

- What kinds of mistakes are people making?
- Why do they think what they do?
- What is getting in the way of their understanding?

Reassemble the group and share insights from the discussions.

2. Dramatize a television talk show. Ask volunteers to play the host and the guests. Guests can include Jesus, the Canaanite woman, and one or two of the disciples. Distribute index cards and ask group members to write out questions for the host to ask each of the guests, for example:
   - To the Canaanite woman: Why didn't you give up and go away?
   - To the disciples: What did you expect Jesus to do when you asked him to send the woman way?
   - To Jesus: What was going through your mind when she turned your own argument against you?

After the presentation, discuss:
   - In what ways does looking at the story from the different points of view enhance our understanding?
   - What new perspectives do we gain?

3. Lead group members in a guided meditation. Invite them to close their eyes and to listen carefully while you read aloud the story of Jesus feeding the multitudes (14:13-21). After the reading, suggest:
   - Picture your surroundings, imagining as much detail as possible: What is the weather like? Is the terrain grassy? rocky? dry? wet? What do you smell? hear? see?
   - Picture yourself in this scene: Are you one of the crowd? a disciple? What are you doing? feeling? thinking? tasting? What is your reaction as the food is passed around?

Allow a few moments of silence; then quietly invite group members to open their eyes. Distribute paper and pencils and ask group members to sketch or describe some of their thoughts and feelings during the meditation. Invite volunteers to share their experience with the group.

Journal Meditation

Review MATTHEW 13:53-58, 14:34-36 and 15:29-31. Compare the different responses of the various groups of people to Jesus' ministry. With which group do you most identify? Why? How satisfied are you with your response to Jesus?

Stepstone To Prayer

Jesus, you are the Christ, Son of the living God!

Matthew 16:21–18:35
Following The Messiah

MATTHEW NOW FOCUSES on Jesus' relationship with the disciples. Steadily Jesus draws his followers into greater understanding of God's self-revelation. This section covers the remainder of the fourth narrative section of Matthew's gospel (16:22–7:27) and the fourth discourse (chap. 18). Read MATTHEW 16:21–18:35.

Find The Facts

What new topic does Jesus introduce? What can followers of Jesus expect? What happens on the high mountain? Who is Jesus teaching in chapter 18? What is his main topic?

Consider:

1. Why do you think Jesus changes the direction of his teaching at this point?

2. What happens to Peter in this passage? With which of his experiences do you most identify?

3. Note phrases that show the major themes of the discourse in chapter 18. What title would you give to chapter 18?

Matthew 16:21-28

The phrase "from that time" indicates a new phase of ministry (Compare 4:17.) Now that the disciples know who Jesus is (16:16), Jesus wants them to understand that his messiahship includes suffering and death even though he is God's own Son. This was a shocking idea to people who had been expecting a triumphant and powerful Messiah. Peter recoils in horror; surely the route of suffering and death is contradictory to Jesus' recent revelation as transcendent Son and Messiah. Jesus' harsh rebuke brings us up short, as it must have done to Peter. Jesus has struggled before with the temptation to use his power for earthly glory (3:10); indeed the image painted by the tempter in chapter 3 is much closer to Peter's probable image of the Messiah than to the vulnerable victim described by Jesus. Ironically, Peter (the Rock) continues to think like the majority of the Jews and thus becomes a "hindrance" (Gk. stumbling stone).

In verse 24 Jesus discusses the implications for disciples of a suffering Messiah. Following Jesus is a serious and possibly dangerous undertaking; for those disciples it may quite literally mean death on a cross. The cross is not the end, however, but the way to the glory of the Father. Paradoxically, losing one's life becomes saving one's life as Jesus turns all human conceptions of loss and gain upside down.

Consider:

4. *What would Christianity be like without the cross? In what ways is the temptation to ignore or avoid pain and suffering appealing? In what ways does your Christian faith help you face up to their reality?*

5. Why do you think Peter reacted as he did? Why did Jesus call him Satan? To what extent do you sympathize with Peter in his rejection of the necessity of Jesus' death in Jerusalem? How do you yourself understand the connection between pain/death and celebration/resurrection?

6. What does it mean to deny yourself and follow Jesus? How does getting rid of self-centeredness open us up to new life? What in your own life do you need to deny (give up) in order to grow as a disciple?

Matthew 17:1-23

The transfiguration confronts us with the full mystery of Christ. Climbing up on a mountain, the now familiar symbol of revelation, the three disciples witness a transformation that puts Jesus' impending death into perspective with the triumphant resurrection. In the Old Testament, both Moses and Elijah (who represent the law and the prophets) receive revelation from God on Sinai. The transfiguration experience shows Jesus in relationship with, yet moving beyond, these heroes of the past.

The voice from the cloud repeats exactly the words spoken at Jesus' baptism, "This is my beloved Son, with whom I am well pleased," adding the injunction, "Listen to him!" We recall how frequently Jesus has said something like, "If you have ears, hear me!" The disciples quite naturally react with fear at the awesome experience, but Jesus calms them with a touch.

As Jesus and the three disciples return from the mountain, Jesus warns them not to speak of their experience until after the events in Jerusalem have played themselves out. Indeed, the disciples themselves do not yet know how to interpret what has happened. They question Jesus about Elijah whose expected return was to signal the new age. Jesus recalls the martyrdom of John the Baptist, pointing out that a similar fate awaits him. This is how uncomprehending humans treat prophets.

Returning to the crowds, Jesus learns that the other disciples have been unable to cast out the demons that plague the epileptic boy. After taking care of the needs of the child, Jesus uses the occasion to lead all the disciples still further into the mysteries of faith. As yet they have "little," but he continues to teach them that even the tiniest bit of faith has great potential. The disciples must learn to trust God's power and not to worry about their own.

7. Why do you think Matthew places the story of the transfiguration right after Jesus reveals his earthly destiny? How does this story change our perspective on Jesus' impending crucifixion? In what ways do you think the experience helped the disciples grow in faith? In what ways does the story help you?

8. Compare 17:19-21 with 14:31. What do you think was getting in the way of the disciples' faith in these episodes? How much faith does Jesus say we need in order to do great things? In what ways might the fear that our faith is insufficient be a barrier to our spiritual growth?

Matthew 17:24–18:14

The story about the payment of taxes bridges the preceding narrative and the discourse on life within the body of believers. Jesus moves to Capernaum where local tax collectors want to know if he will pay the temple taxes or claim exemption like the priests and rabbis sometimes did. Jesus explains that, though the sons of the Father are free from such obligation, because of the law of love (5:43-48) and the necessity to live in peace with others, the tax should be paid. Jesus miraculously supplies the coin by asking Peter to go fishing.

Jesus' teaching on humility and forgiveness in chapter 18 deals with life and discipline among his followers. Christian communities need to be caring communities in which members grow in faith and equip each other for the task of discipleship. Verses 1-14 discuss caring in terms of children and little ones.

Who is the greatest? The disciples are once more on the wrong track; yet Jesus patiently instructs them, this time through a startling example. Children were not romanticized at that time; they were pieces of property with no rights. To become like a child would be to voluntarily take a position of extreme vulnerability. Greatness in the kingdom will be for those who admit their littleness before God and have an attitude of childlike (not childish) trust. To receive such a humble person because of Jesus is like receiving Jesus himself. Greatness in the kingdom will also be reserved for those who care for these "little ones" who may actually be children, or who may be adults immature or weak in faith. Such care may involve bringing strays back to the fold (vv. 10-14) or not tempting anyone to sin (literally "to cause to stumble"). Better death by drowning than a careless attitude toward those whose faith is still fragile (vv. 6-9)! Temptations will surely come (v. 7), but those who tempt others stand in grave danger of judgment.

The parable of the lost sheep further illustrates God's loving concern for each individual. Within the Church we must exhibit a similar concern. Contempt for those who stray is wrong. Rather, church leaders must be like the shepherd who finds greater joy in caring for the sheep outside the fold than in tending those safely within. Jesus also expects us to acknowledge and include the little ones of this world.

9. What is the difference between being childish and being childlike? What childlike qualities do you think Jesus has in mind? What are some ways to reclaim these as adults? How can the children in our families or communities help us in this endeavor?

10. Why is causing someone else to stumble a serious sin? Why do we need to show special care to those who are new or immature in the faith? What are some ways to help others grow in faith? What techniques has Jesus been using to help the disciples grow in faith?

11. In your own experience, why do people leave our church communities? According to 10-14, what should be our attitude toward them? What are some ways to invite them back? What kind of "shepherding" might they need before they are ready to return?

Matthew 18:15-35

Jesus now turns to the subject of Christians who sin against one another. Forgiveness among members stands as a basic principle of the church community, but even compassion has its limits. Divisive wrongdoing cannot be ignored but calls for sensitive correction. An offender who persists in the face of all efforts becomes like a despised tax collector or a Gentile. Though the Church has seen this passage as the basis for the practice of excommunication, we might note that Jesus himself has shown consistent and particular concern for these categories of outcasts.

Verse 20 emphasizes the power of collective prayer. A Jewish tradition held that wherever two people discussed the law, the *shekinah* (divine presence) was with them. Fidelity to Jesus assures his presence to believers (1:23).

Peter's question in verse 21 brings us back to the main theme, forgiveness—the key to Christian community. Seventy times seven becomes a number representative of limitless forgiveness. Jesus reinforces his reply with a parable. The servant who fails to learn from his own experience of forgiveness and refuses to forgive a fellow servant receives severe judgment. The final verse emphasizes the need to share the forgiveness we have received with others and recalls the Lord's Prayer: "Forgive us our debts, As we also have forgiven our debtors" (6:12).

Consider:

12. Why is forgiveness important in the Christian community? How are persistent offenders dealt with in your church community? How difficult do you find it to confront another with wrongdoing? Why do you think Jesus suggests this approach in verses 15-18?

13. Rabbis of Jesus' day taught that one should forgive three times for the same offense, but not a fourth time. How does Jesus' reply to Peter's question change this principle? How do you reconcile verse 22 with verse 17? Where do you experience the tension between the need to forgive and the need to discipline?

14. What does it mean to forgive "from the heart" (v. 35)? What wisdom do you see in the folk adage "forgive and forget"? What wrongs against you would you like to forget?

Group Activities

1. Divide into small groups of three or four. Pass around magazines, newspapers, scissors, glue and poster board. Using illustrations, ads, cartoons, headlines, etc., make a collage that illustrates some qualities of small children, for example, joy, trust or vulnerability. Share the collages in the large group and discuss: How are these examples representative of the kind of humility that Jesus is talking about in MATTHEW 18:4?

2. Invite a volunteer to read aloud MATTHEW 18:12-14. After the reading, discuss:

   • What happens in our church community when a member leaves?
   • According to this parable, which do you think should receive the greater emphasis: caring for those who remain in the community or caring for those who leave it?

   List on newsprint, whiteboard or chalkboard some of the reasons you think people leave your community. In a parallel column list some ideas for bringing them back. Underline the ones that sound realistic and discuss putting some of your ideas into action.

3. Distribute paper and pencils. Ask group members to reflect quietly—in writing, if they wish—on the values discussed in MATTHEW 18.

   After several minutes, list group members' ideas on chalkboard, whiteboard or newsprint and try to identify some concrete ways to implement them in daily life. After a few minutes, invite group members to turn to another person and share whatever parts of their reflection they choose to talk about.

   Reassemble the group and discuss:
   • What difficulties do we encounter as we apply Christian values in our workplaces? in our families?
   • What helps us to apply these values?
   • In what ways can we help each other?

Journal Meditation

Reread MATTHEW 17:1-8. When have you experienced God in a special and unusual way? It need not be as dramatic as the experience of Peter, James and John, but rather a time that was special to you. What was it like? How did you feel afterward? In the space below describe or sketch your memory of the occasion.

Stepstone To Prayer

God, help me to approach you with childlike trust.

Matthew 19–20
Journey to Jerusalem

THE FAMILIAR FORMULA of 19:1 marks the end of the preceding discourse and signals the beginning of the fifth narrative section of Matthew's gospel. On the road to Jerusalem Jesus meets both hecklers and sincere petitioners. He responds to each according to their unique needs, using these opportunities to instruct his disciples. Read MATTHEW 19–20.

Find The Facts

Where does the action take place? Where are Jesus and the disciples going? What does Jesus do along the way? What people question Jesus? What subjects do they ask him about?

Consider:

1. What do you think is most significant about Jesus' discussion of marriage and divorce? Why?

2. What are some of the demands and rewards of discipleship?

Matthew 19:1-15

The narrative resumes with a shift in geographical location. After the preparation begun in 16:21, Jesus and the disciples now enter Judea and physically move toward Jerusalem. As they travel, Jesus encounters a variety of petitioners—Pharisees, children, a rich young man, the mother of James and John, and two blind men.

Jesus first meets the Pharisees, who still hope to catch him contradicting the law of Moses. The Pharisees question Jesus about divorce. Jesus uses a recognized rabbinical method of argument ("the more original, the weightier") as he appeals to God's original purpose in creating female and male, citing GENESIS 1:27 and 2:24. This does not necessarily negate Moses' law, but puts it into perspective. Moses provided rules for divorce (DT. 24:1ff) not because of the desirability of the practice, but because of the sinful behavior of the people. God's original intention was for lasting union between the sexes. Divorce, though sometimes necessary, violates the created order.

The disciples then exclaim that such restrictions make marriage less attractive; perhaps one should avoid it altogether. Jesus points out that the celibate life is given to some from birth, forced on some through circumstance, and chosen by some who renounce marriage in order to put all their energies toward service of the kingdom.

In contrast to the crafty Pharisees, the next people who approach Jesus are innocent children. Jesus reminds the impatient disciples that children are the very essence of the kingdom (see 18:1-4), and he interrupts his journey in order to bless them.

Consider:

3. In what ways does Matthew 5:20 illuminate Jesus' response to the Pharisees' question about lawful divorce? How is Jesus' appeal to something more fundamental than the intricacies of the law typical of much of his teaching in this gospel?

4. How has divorce affected your life or that of your family? How do you feel about the basic principle that marriage is meant to be a lifelong union? Do you think this ideal makes marriage more or less attractive? Why? Do you agree that celibacy is the only alternative? For what reasons might a person choose celibacy?

Matthew 19:16-26

This section continues to explore the cost of discipleship (16:24). Just as Jesus called for a high ideal of marriage, one that goes beyond the technical requirements of the law, he now calls for a morality that goes beyond adherence to specific laws.

Jesus' next petitioner, a wealthy young man, addresses Jesus as "teacher." The use of this title suggests an immature understanding of Jesus' identity. (Compare 20:31.) The young man asks Jesus about doing a good deed, perhaps referring to the Jewish practice of doing good deeds beyond the strict demands of the law to insure entrance into heaven. Jesus replies that the good God has already given clear commandments for a good life. The young man persists in his demand for an exact formula, adding that he observes the commandments but still lacks something. To be perfect, that is, to serve God with wholehearted dedication, means to go beyond the law, not through specific good deeds but through getting rid of whatever stands between the individual and Christ. To the young man who had great possessions Jesus says, "Get rid of everything you possess and follow me." The young man goes away sorrowful as he realizes he cannot serve God and mammon (6:24).

Jesus uses this occasion to point out to the disciples how difficult it is for rich people to be saved; as in the case of the young man, their possessions are likely to possess them. The example he chooses actually represents an impossibility (v. 24). The disciples are astonished because people generally believed that wealth is a sign of God's favor. If the wealthy cannot be saved, who can? Verse 26 repeats the good news that all people, rich and poor, can be saved through the free gift of God, not through their own efforts.

5. Which of the Beatitudes (5:1-11) do you think of when you hear this story? To what extent do you think it is possible for one who has "great possessions" to be "poor in spirit" (humble)? Besides material possessions, what can stand between an individual and total dedication to God?

6. In what way does this story of the young man invite us to reflect on our own faith journeys? In your life, what possessions, habits, etc., have you needed to abandon in order to follow Jesus? What are some current stumbling blocks to your progress? What is your next step?

Matthew 19:27—20:16

The disciples, as Peter quickly points out, have actually done what Jesus recommended to the rich young man. They have given up everything they have in order to follow Jesus. In response to Peter's blunt question, Jesus assures the disciples they will receive the eternal life that the rich young man found too costly (19:29). Jesus tells the disciples that their reward will include sharing authority in the new age. "Judging" here means governing or ruling. The twelve are the foundations on which Jesus will build the new Israel.

A second promise to all disciples, not just the twelve, assures us that all true followers will share in a rich inheritance. Discipleship involves giving up much that is valuable in human terms, but promises the disciple a reward of indescribable value in God's terms. In God's kingdom, ordinary human values are reversed. Many who are first in the present scheme of things (Pharisees, rich youths) will be last in the new order. Likewise those who now hold lowly positions (the disciples, the poor, the children) will be first in the kingdom.

Jesus then tells a parable to illustrate the paradoxical concept that the first will be last and the last first. The parable about the laborers in the vineyard is not a commentary on economic justice, but an illustration of the boundless generosity of God. Knowing the immense power of a first-century Palestinian landowner, Jesus compares this powerful position to God's freedom to dispense gifts where God wills. The rewards of discipleship are not earned, but given (19:26). Begrudging God's generosity is inappropriate. There is enough for all.

Consider:

7. *What reward does Jesus promise to faithful disciples? What does it mean to you to put God first, even before family and property? How does this priority put your other responsibilities in perspective?*

8. *With which group of laborers do you most identify, the ones who worked a full day or those who came last and received just as much pay? Why?*

9. *In what ways does this parable challenge us to reexamine our understanding of what is just and fair? Which is more appropriate—to begrudge those who do not have to work as hard as we do to enter the kingdom or to feel thankful to God for the gracious love that extends to all? What are some ways to imitate God's loving generosity?*

Matthew 20:17-28

This section begins with another reminder that Jesus is drawing nearer to Jerusalem. The third passion prediction is more detailed than 16:21 or 17:22 and provides a concise summary of the whole passion narrative to follow. Coming as it does after the discussion of rewards, it reinforces the theme of reversal. Death for Jesus will be followed by resurrection.

The next petitioner is another person who does not yet grasp the full import of Jesus' teaching. The mother of James and John reverently and earnestly approaches Jesus with the request that her sons have places of honor in the coming kingdom. Jesus explains that sharing his position of honor means sharing his suffering also. Even so, God, not Jesus, bestows honor.

The other disciples betray their own pettiness when they hear of the episode, and, as in 18:1-5, Jesus uses the occasion to present an important teaching. He defines greatness in terms of service. Unlike the pagan Gentiles who function in a hierarchical system of authority and servitude, followers of Jesus will all be as slaves to one another. Jesus himself is the role model of this high ideal of service; he will give everything, even his life. Jesus, who rejected power in the way the world understood it (4:1-11), chooses to express his power through service.

Consider:

10. How does the episode between Jesus and the mother of James and John shed further light on Jesus' paradoxical saying in 20:16? Compare 18:1-4. What do children and servants have in common?

11. Why do you think the ten other disciples were indignant (v. 24)? When do you feel indignant in your own Christian community? What sort of antidote is suggested by verses 25-28? How would focusing on service to others improve some of your personal relationships?

Matthew 20:29-34

James, John and the other disciples have demonstrated their blindness in failing to understand the scope and meaning of Jesus' passion. The Pharisees and a rich young man have also been blind. Hence the placement of this story seems significant. The reversal is obvious: it is the blind who see. The blind "recognize" Jesus, calling him Son of David, the most popular messianic name. As if to emphasize their importance, we have not one, but two blind beggars crying out to Jesus as he passes on his way out of Jericho. Perhaps Matthew provides two blind men because of the Jewish tradition that a minimum of two are necessary to corroborate testimony. Jesus, who comes "not to be served but to serve" responds in pity. He heals and they follow.

Consider:

12. *How would you compare the blindness of the two men in Jericho with the blindness of the disciples (vv. 20-28)? Which group would you expect to have greater understanding of Jesus at this point? In your own life, who are some of the people who have surprised you by their unexpected insight?*

Group Activities

1. Review MATTHEW 19:16-22 together. Divide into small groups and invite groups to discuss what might have happened next. The man who went away sorrowful was young. What do you think the rest of his life was like? Where did he go? What did he do? Did he tell anyone what happened? Who? What was his version of the story? What were his great possessions? What did he do with them? How did his encounter with Jesus affect him over time?

   Allow 10 to 15 minutes for discussion, then reassemble the group and invite volunteers to share their groups' conclusions.

2. In the context of MATTHEW 20:28 and 34, discuss the needs of your church's neighborhood (or town or county):
   • In what ways does your congregation present Christ as a servant to the community?

   On newsprint, whiteboard or newsprint list the needs that group members identify. Check off the ones that you feel are already being addressed. Select one or two others and brainstorm ways your community can be of service in these areas.

3. Distribute paper and pencils. Ask members to list individually the names of people who are good models of discipleship. After a few minutes form groups of three or four and share lists. Discuss:
   • What are the characteristics of contemporary disciples?
   • Which characteristics are most difficult to live out in our competitive society?
   • What are some ways in which Christians can help each other develop these qualities?

   Reassemble the group and share insights from the small-group discussions.

Journal Meditation

Reflect on MATTHEW 20:32. How would you feel if Jesus asked how he could serve you? How might you respond? The blind men used an image of restored sight. What image is most meaningful to you in terms of your own needs? In the space below sketch or describe the way you want to respond to Jesus' question, "What do you want me to do for you?"

Stepstone To Prayer

Lord, let my eyes be opened.

Matthew 21–23
The Messiah's Authority

AT LAST JESUS AND THE DISCIPLES reach their destination. This section covers the entry into Jerusalem and events that take place in the temple soon thereafter. Read MATTHEW 21–23.

Find The Facts

What kind of welcome does Jesus receive from the crowds? What does Jesus do first after his arrival in Jerusalem? Who challenges Jesus' authority? What are some of their particular concerns? How does Jesus deal with his challengers? What is his final word about them?

1. *What significance do you see in the method Jesus chooses for his entrance into Jerusalem?*

2. *Underline key phrases that deal with the question of Jesus' authority.*

3. *Compare the mood of Matthew 23:37-39 with 21:1-11.*

Matthew 21:1-17

As soon as their destination is in sight, Jesus gives an order; the disciples rush to obey. We sense a new surge of energy as the events we celebrate during Holy Week begin. Matthew quotes the prophet Zechariah (v. 5) to explain the somewhat peculiar preparations. This playing out of the messianic prophecy (ZECH. 9:9) will be the first public proclamation of Jesus as Messiah. (In his zeal to report the prophecy fulfilled in all respects, Matthew has Jesus riding on two animals. In the original text the phrase "a colt, the foal of an ass" merely describes one animal a second time.)

The crowds, familiar with the prophecy, get the message immediately and hail Jesus as the Son of David, the Messiah. The shout of "Hosanna" is more than praise; it means "save, now!" "Blessed is he who comes in the name of the Lord" has liturgical significance for us today, but during Jesus' time it was the standard greeting to the pilgrims who entered the holy city. Word spreads rapidly through the city, which is unusually crowded because of the approaching feast of Passover. Pilgrims, coming to the feast, throng the roads and answer the question, "Who is this (that is called Son of David)?"

Jesus goes directly to the temple, the heart of Judaism and the center of activity in the city. He immediately sets about overturning the old order. The outer court of the temple was known as the Court of the Gentiles; things necessary for sacrifice—animals, birds, wine, salt, oil, etc.—were for sale; and money-changers were prepared to change the pilgrims' Greek and Roman coins into the temple coins necessary to make their purchases and pay the temple tax. All this activity prevented the Gentiles from worshiping in the only area of the temple where they were allowed. In verse 13 Jesus quotes ISAIAH 56:7. Oddly, Matthew omits the words "for all peoples" (see MK. 11:17), which help explain Jesus' motive in clearing out the courtyard. After driving out the money changers and salesmen, Jesus proceeds to heal the outcasts who have followed him into the temple. The chief priests and scribes are indignant, but the children recognize Jesus (Ps. 8:2; MT. 19:14).

Consider:

4. Why do you think Jesus decides at this time to announce publicly that he is the Messiah? In what sense is this the point of no return for Jesus? What might have been his thoughts as he rode through the cheering crowds? What kinds of feelings do you have when you contemplate proclaiming Christ publicly?

5. What do Jesus' actions in the temple tell us about him? about his values? about his call for true worship? In your life, when do you let the formalities of worship interfere with its real purpose?

Matthew 21:18-27

Jesus returns to Jerusalem after spending the night in Bethany. Some commentators describe the curious incident of the fig tree (18-22) as a parable-in-action. Some classify it as a miracle, but Jesus' miracles normally help, heal or save. In either case the symbolism is clear. The fig tree represents Pharisaic Judaism, which is covered with plenty of "leafy" ostentatious piety but lacks the fruit of true religion. In the normal growing cycle, fruit would appear before the leaves on a fig tree. The disciples marvel at the withered tree. Jesus returns to the theme of doubt vs. faith (17:20; 14:31) and reassures them about the power of the prayers of the faithful.

Verses 23-27 introduce the critical question of Jesus' authority. He enters the temple as he did the preceding day, but this time he begins to teach. The chief priests (those in control of the temple, mostly Sadducees) interrupt his teaching to pose the $64,000 question. Jesus counters with a question that puts his challengers on the spot. To say that John's baptism came from God would be to convict themselves of failure to repent; to say that it was merely human would get them in trouble with the commoners who hailed John as a martyred prophet. Like many other public officials throughout history, they hedge. Jesus then refuses to carry the dispute further, but he has publicly demonstrated his superiority over the false teachers. They will not forget nor forgive this embarrassment.

Consider:

6. How do you see the incident of the fig tree serving as a parable for what has already happened in the temple? for what happens in verses 23-27? What does it teach about prayer, religious practices, faith, values and priorities? Where are your own priorities regarding religious practices?

Matthew 21:28—22:14

Jesus resumes his teaching by telling three parables about the judgment of Israel. Note the chief priests and the Pharisees are still part of the audience (21:45). Though Jesus has refused to continue the dispute about his authority, the parables make clear the consequences for those who fail to recognize it.

The first parable makes the simple point that actions speak louder than words. Better to repent and obey than to promise obedience and do nothing about it. Jesus drives home the point with his reference to the repentant tax collectors and harlots, who enter the kingdom of God before the respectable people who ignored John's message.

In the second parable, unfaithful tenants tend Israel, God's vineyard. They reject two sets of servants sent to claim the owner's harvest and then murder the owner's son. Israel has not heeded its prophets in the past and is about to crucify the Messiah. Therefore, Jesus says, the kingdom will be offered to a new "nation" (those who will produce fruits).

Needless to say the listening leaders are angry, but they are afraid to arrest Jesus in front of the enthusiastic crowds. So Jesus tells a third parable, which continues the idea that God's kingdom will be offered to those who are able to respond to the invitation, both good and bad. The harsh treatment of the guest who comes improperly attired warns the Christian community against a complacent attitude about what is required for a welcome in God's kingdom; those within the Church are also subject to judgment.

7. Which of the three parables speaks to you most clearly about the need to respond to God's call? In what ways can you apply its teachings to your spiritual situation?

8. In what ways do we do violence to the servants that God sends to the Church (vv. 34-36)? In what ways do we do violence to Jesus, God's Son (vv. 37-39)?

9. In what forms does God's invitation come to people today? What is the role of the Church in issuing the invitation? In helping those who respond to be "properly dressed" for participation?

Matthew 22:15-46

Verse 15 resumes the series of dispute stories begun in 21:23-27. The Pharisees, who do not give in easily, enlist members of Herod's party in their next attempt at verbal entrapment. The tax mentioned in verse 17 was a poll tax levied on all males over 14 and all females over 12 throughout the provinces of Roman rule. The Herodians, naturally, supported the tax; the Pharisees opposed it. They have phrased a question designed to make Jesus offend one group or the other. His answer is a clever technique, but probably also reflects a genuine acknowledgment of the claims of civil government as long as they do not conflict with the claims of God.

Next the Sadducees pose a complicated question based on an ancient law of the levirate (brother-in-law). Sadducees, who did not believe in the resurrection of the dead because they rejected any concept not found in the Pentateuch, cite passages (Dt. 25:5, Gen. 38:8) that reflect the primitive belief that immortality comes through progeny, hence the importance of the continuance of the dead man's line. Their question assumes that if there is resurrection it is a miraculous return to bodily life on earth. Jesus' reply thus addresses the real issue of resurrection rather than the hypothetical case. He explains that resurrection is not a coming back, but a going forward to something new where the physical and sexual relationships of this world are transcended. He cites Exodus 3:6: Abraham, Isaac and Jacob are long dead; yet they live because of their faith. God is the God of the living!

The Pharisees try one more time: "What is the greatest commandment?" In reply Jesus quotes the Shema, the ancient Hebrew prayer (Dt. 6:4-5). He summarizes the law and the prophets by combining the two great commandments: love of God and love of neighbor. Jesus makes this combination the basis for our ethical code (5:17; 7:12).

In the last of these dispute stories, Jesus poses the question to the Pharisees. They do believe the Messiah will be the son of David; Matthew's gospel has consistently presented this view along with the idea of son of David and something more—son of God. Jesus' explanation to the Pharisees reflects this and indeed silences his opponents at last. He has bested them in all disputes and they do not dare to ask him any more questions.

10. How do we distinguish today between what is "Caesar's" and what is "God's"? What do you think Jesus is teaching about our obligations to Church and state (v. 21)? What is it that should be given to God?

11. How is love the basis for all the "law and the prophets"? How does the combination of the two great commandments (love of God and love of others as of self) provide the link between religious faith and ethics (behavior)? What is the relationship between loving God, loving others and loving self? Is one of them primary? Why or why not?

Matthew 23

Chapter 23 is the climax to the series of disputes. The challengers have been silenced (22:46) and Jesus speaks. First he warns the crowds and the disciples about scribes and Pharisees (23:1-12); then he passionately condemns hypocritical practices (13-36); finally he laments over Jerusalem.

Jesus opens his remarks with a reference to "Moses' seat," a stone seat in the front of the synagogue, where the authoritative teacher sat. Jesus' main objection to the scribes and the Pharisees is not their teaching, but their hypocrisy. They do not observe their own teaching (v. 3). They invite public acclaim by ostentatiously wearing broad phylacteries (two small boxes containing scriptures [DT. 11:18], one strapped on the forehead and the other strapped to the upper left arm) and long fringes (tassels attached to garments as reminders to obey God's commandments [NUM. 15:38-40]). They order their own lives to suit themselves, but lay heavy burdens on the people. Jesus wants the people to be free of these demands.

Followers of Jesus will model a different way: all members of God's family are equals; no one may claim authority over others as teacher. (In Matthew's time, scribes were officially called rabbi, meaning teacher, father or master, vv. 8-10.)

Jesus stressed the virtue of humility and directs scathing criticism to the leaders he calls hypocrites. This chapter should not be regarded as a balanced critique of Pharisaism as a whole. Matthew was writing for the early Church and was probably concerned that any institution can fall into the trap of "saying" without "doing." The chapter thus represents warnings for Church leaders throughout history as well as Jesus' judgment on the hypocrisy of his time.

In prophetic and apocalyptic literature, "woe" expresses both dismay and threat of punishment. Jesus pronounces seven woes:

- First, such hypocrites hinder entrance into the kingdom instead of facilitating it (vv. 13-14).

- Second, in their excessive zeal for converts, hypocrites merely perpetuate their own kind (v. 15).

- Third, hypocrites give too much attention to elaborate distinctions between different kinds of oaths and thus dilute and confuse the true intent of the law (vv. 16-22).

- Fourth, and in the same vein, tithing of vegetables and spices represents excessive zeal for minutiae, leading to the neglect of more important matters (vv. 23-24).

- Fifth, the Pharisaic custom of ritual washing of vessels becomes a metaphor for their misguided concern with externals (vv. 25-26).

- The sixth woe extends this contrast between concern for the external and internal. Pharisees taught that any kind of contact with the dead transmitted impurity, so tombs were whitewashed. Jesus says hypocrites are like these tombs, beautiful on the outside (ostentatious behavior), but corrupt within (vv. 27-28).

- In the seventh woe, Jesus suggests that the Pharisees, the physical sons of those who murdered the prophets, are their spiritual sons as well (vv. 29-36). Early Jewish Christians suffered considerable persecution from overzealous Pharisees (v. 34).

His righteous indignation vented, Jesus' tone changes dramatically as he mourns for Jerusalem, which suffers greatly for its blind rejection of true guides.

Consider:

12. Compare 23:2-4 with 11:28-30. What is the burden that Pharisees lay on the people? In what ways is Jesus' yoke easy and his burden light in comparison? What burden are you carrying now that is too heavy? How does Jesus' advice suggest a way to lighten it?

13. Underline the word *blind* each time it appears in the text. What are the things that the Pharisees cannot see? What prevents their seeing? What kinds of things today distract us from our true values and priorities? In your own life, about what unnecessary details are you overzealous?

14. What do you see in common among the seven "woes"? In your own words write a summary of the woes. In what ways would you like them to be taken seriously by the Church today?

Group Activities

1. Divide into groups of three or four. Imagine that Jesus is planning to enter your city today to announce his messiahship. How would you go about

making sure people got the message? What media would you use? what words to state the message? what nonverbal means of communication? Let each group develop a public relations plan for announcing the event. Share the plans, and discuss:

- What do these scenarios suggest about effective evangelism in our own time?

- Consider the change in the Jerusalem crowd's attitude as Jesus continues in the city. What prevents people today from following through on their commitment to Christ?

2. Read MATTHEW 22:11-13. If we assume that Jesus is not concerned with what kind of clothing we wear, what was the offense of the guest who had no wedding garment?

   Brainstorm together and record the group's ideas on newsprint, whiteboard or chalkboard:

   - What constitutes appropriate preparation for participation in God's kingdom?

   - What kinds of attitudes, values and priorities do we need to develop?

   - Compare your list to MATTHEW 5:1-11.

3. Compare MATTHEW 5:20 WITH 23:8-12. In groups of three or four discuss:

   - Why does Jesus demand more of his own followers than of the acknowledged leaders of the religious community?

   - Based on 23:8-12, how should our own church communities function?

   - What are some good role models?

4. Review MATTHEW 23:33-38. Pass around pencils and paper and ask group members to reflect individually on these questions:

   - What would be Jesus' comment on your own city/community today?

   - What would cause Jesus to feel sorrowful?

   - What might Jesus find that gives him joy?

   After a few minutes, invite group members to each share their insights with one other person. In the same pairs compose a prayer for your city/community. Post the prayers.

Journal Meditation

Read MATTHEW 22:37. What does it mean to love God with all your heart? with all your soul? with all your mind? How is each different from the others? Why are all three needed? Use the space below to sketch or describe loving God with all your heart, all your soul and all your mind.

Stepstone To Prayer

Help me to experience the joy and blessing of the One who comes in the name of the Lord.

Matthew 24–25
The Vision of Things to Come

I N THE FIFTH AND FINAL DISCOURSE of his gospel, Matthew presents Jesus' teachings about the future. Like the Sermon on the Mount (chaps. 5-7) this discourse is most likely a collection of sayings woven together by the skillful writer. Much of the language is drawn from the Old Testament apocalyptic writings that depict symbolically the ultimate destruction of evil and triumph of good. Though familiar to readers of Matthew's time, these writings often seem obscure and difficult to us today. The text itself hints that it is something like a code to be deciphered (24:15).

The apocalyptic style of writing is usually found in periods of history characterized by conflict, oppression and tension. Often the purpose is to offer hope and encouragement to oppressed and persecuted people in a highly symbolic form the oppressors will not understand. Frequently such writings take the form of a vision in which a hero or prophet predicts events in the future, usually including some that readers would recognize as already having occurred. Some examples from the Hebrew Scriptures are Daniel, Ezekiel and Zechariah. With this in mind, read MATTHEW 24–25.

Find The Facts

What is the setting for this discourse? To whom is Jesus speaking? What is his main concern? What parables does he tell? Upon what will the final judgment be based?

Consider:

1. What question do the disciples ask? Why is this an appropriate time for Jesus to talk with his disciples about the future?

2. Note the passages or phrases that you do not understand. What are your questions about them?

3. Which of Jesus' stories speaks to you most deeply? Why?

Matthew 24:1-35

After uttering his sorrowful lament over Jerusalem (23:37-39), Jesus leaves the temple. The disciples call attention to the impressive temple structures, which Jesus sees as representative of power that rejects God. He knows that they are doomed. Indeed, in A.D. 70 the Romans destroyed the temple and the city, so by the time this gospel was being written Jesus' prophecy had literally been fulfilled.

In this discourse, teachings about the destruction of the temple merge with details from the Old Testament associated with the end of human history. According to the Jewish concept of the "day of the Lord," time is divided into two ages—the present age and the age to come. The evils of the present age can be mended only by God's direct action. When God intervenes, the age to come will arrive. But in between will come the day of the Lord, a terrifying time of cosmic upheaval and moral chaos. The fearful images of verses 6-8 and 29-31 reflect this concept.

Verse 3 sets the scene for the fifth and last discourse. Sitting on the Mount of Olives, a site associated with the coming of the day of the Lord (ZECH. 14:4), Jesus answers his disciples' anxious questions about the future. When will this (your coming, that is, *parousia*) be? What will be the sign of your coming? What will be the sign of the close of the age?

Jesus sees two dangers that will threaten the faith of believers in the times to come: false leaders and discouragement. He warns against these in verses 4-5, 11-13 and 23-26. False leaders are those who attempt to draw people to themselves rather than to Christ; they thus create disunity rather than unity. The distressing events in the world will cause the love of some to grow cold. The true follower will trust God's love and endure to the end.

The images in verses 6-8 reflect the Old Testament understanding of the coming of the Son of man (DAN. 7:13). In this last act of world history would come the institution of the reign of God and the subjection of all hostile powers. The early Christian tradition quite naturally associated these images of the long foretold day of the Lord with Jesus' second coming or *parousia* (Gk. word meaning arrival, presence; used by Matthew to mean Jesus' final and glorious coming at the end of history). Jesus, as Savior and Judge, will then reign supreme. Verses 6 and 7 chronicle the expected violence between peoples and in the created order (previously accepted signs of the close of the age). Yet, verse 8 emphasizes that what may seem like chaos is actually the beginning of the new creation.

Followers of Christ will be persecuted, some will fall away, but those who endure to the end will be saved (vv. 9-13). In spite of the tribulations, the gospel message will spread through the world; when this momentous task has been accomplished, the end will be achieved.

The desolating sacrilege known to the Jews was when Antiochus Epiphanes profaned the temple with his pagan god (DAN. 7:27). Verses 16-20 describe the suddenness with which the new age will come, requiring prompt response. Another warning against false prophets is followed by the reassurance that when the Son of man comes, it will not be a secret; everyone will know it. It will be like lightning, an image that conveys brilliance of appearance as well as sudden arrival (v. 17). Signs in the heavens (v. 29; AM. 8:9) will herald the *parousia* (v. 30; DAN. 7:13-14) and the triumphant Christ will gather all the faithful from throughout the world (v. 31). Use of these familiar metaphors affirms the inevitable end of history without giving any precise information. As certainly as the fig tree gives clear signs that summer is near, we can trust the words of Jesus (vv. 32-35).

Consider:

4. *Why do you think Jesus is concerned that people would be led astray? When in history have people been eager to follow a false leader? If we are not to trust the false prophets, whom are we to trust? To whom do you go when you need clarity of direction?*

5. What is your response to Jesus' description of "wars and rumors of wars" and all kinds of natural disasters as "birthpangs"? When there is chaos in our lives, how do we typically respond? How does believing that chaos is the stuff of new beginnings help us to avoid discouragement?

6. What does verse 14 suggest we should be doing while in the midst of multiple wickedness, wars, famines, etc...? Who does Jesus expect to preach the gospel throughout the world? How well does today's Church bring Jesus' message of peace to the world?

Matthew 14:36-51

In the rest of the fifth discourse, Jesus teaches how to face the uncertainties of the future by alerting us to the reality of his return. We know as little about what lies ahead as did Noah and his family (vv. 37-39).

When the day of the Lord arrives some will be ready and some will not (vv. 40-41). Christians, therefore, need to be vigilant and prepared for judgment at all times. Jesus tells four parables to illustrate his point.

The parable of the householder (42-44) compares the coming of the Son of man to a burglary. The suddenness of the break-in catches the householder off guard. Since we cannot predict the hour of Jesus' coming, we must live in readiness all the time.

The parable of the servant (45-51) emphasizes fidelity. The head of a household will be pleased with the servant who faithfully goes about the work with which he or she is entrusted. But servants who neglect their work and do as they please when the boss is not around will be punished along with the hypocrites when they are caught. The description of the servant, as one set over the other servants with the responsibility of tending to their needs, may mean Matthew had church leaders specifically in mind. The unfaithful Christian leader is no better than the unfaithful Jewish leaders whom Jesus has labeled hypocrites (chap. 23). For Christians, vigilance alone is not enough. There is work to be done!

Consider:

7. *How could the householder have prevented the break-in? With what attitudes are we to wait for the coming of the Son of man?*

Focus on Matthew

8. *What are some of the tasks that Jesus has entrusted to the Church? What sort of work are we to engage in while waiting and watching for the* parousia? *How do you see your own role in this work?*

Matthew 25:1-30

In Palestinian villages even today, a wedding is a momentous occasion. Friends of the bride join with her to prepare and wait for the bridegroom, who may come at any time to take her to his house where the wedding ceremony followed by weeklong festivities will take place. It is something of a game for the bridegroom's party to arrive unexpectedly and catch the bridal party napping. In this context the parable of the ten maidens makes great sense. No one knew exactly how long they would be waiting, so the smart thing to do was have extra oil. Since the foolish ones did not anticipate the possibility of delay, they missed the party. Jesus warns us to be prepared for a delayed arrival *(parousia)*. Oil symbolized good works to Jews, so those who kept themselves busy doing God's work were known to the bridegroom when he came; those who had idled their time away were not recognized.

The fourth parable makes clear the meaning of being watchful and ready. The time of waiting and watching must be filled with active and responsible service, making creative use of God's gifts. In the story a wealthy businessman goes away for a long time; before leaving he divides his capital among three servants, trusting them to keep the business going while he is away. (A talent, originally a measure of weight, here is the largest unit of currency known in the Hellenistic world.) He knows his servants well and distributes responsibility according to their various abilities. Upon his return he is delighted with those who made creative investments and angry with the one who squirreled away the money and took no risk to make it grow.

This latter parable makes several points. God gives different people different gifts; it is not the magnitude of the gift that matters, but how one uses it. The man with only one talent did not misuse the money; his sin was doing nothing; the one who will not try loses the little he has. Those who do their work well do not get to rest on their laurels, but are given yet a greater task. We need to be willing to risk or there is no possibility of growth.

Consider:

9. *What was the probable expectation of the disciples relative to the parousia? What expectation do you think the members of Matthew's early church had? Why do you think Jesus tells a story about being prepared for delay? Which is more important, the end of history or the process of Christian living?*

10. What happens when we focus on a future event and forget the present? How can such an attitude damage relationships, prevent accomplishments, make us generally ineffective? To what do you need to pay more attention in the here and now?

11. When you think of your own God-given gifts, with which of the three servants do you identify most? Why? How great is the task God has given to you? To what extent do you feel it is a reasonable expectation and "according to your ability?"

Matthew 25:31-46

After instructing the disciples about what they are to do while waiting for the *parousia*, Jesus paints a word picture of the final day of reckoning. When that moment comes, judgment will be based on a person's actions. Those who respond in love to human need will be blessed; those who ignore the needs of others will be punished.

Verse 31 paints a majestic picture: Before the throne are gathered all the nations; judgment is being pronounced on all the world, not just Christians. Even in this majestic setting Jesus selects an ordinary, easily understood image. In Palestine, mixed flocks of sheep and goats are common. Shepherds separate them each evening because goats must be kept warm at night. This king is a shepherd who knows his flock.

Just as Israel inherited an earthly promised land, the new people of God (who represent all nations) will inherit the heavenly kingdom. The separation is based on performance of a commonly understood list of good works; the surprise comes when Jesus equates service to "the least of these" (see "the little ones," 10:42) with service to himself. Failure to respond to the poor and needy is failure to respond to Christ himself. Matthew has already pointed out that not all those invited to the banquet will be among the chosen (22:14). What turns the invited into the chosen is a life of practical, daily, loving actions.

Consider:

12. *What does it take to do the things Jesus mentions as important? What sometimes prevents you from doing these things? What other actions toward "the least of these" would you add to Jesus' list? What other "least" individuals might you add? Why?*

13. In this passage, do you think Jesus means that caring for others makes us righteous or that being righteous makes us caring? Or do you think Jesus means something else? Explain.

14. What motivating factors compel us to care for the "least" in our community? in the world? Compare Matthew 22:36–40 with 25:40, 45. How does this story of judgment link together the two commandments that Jesus says are most important? How is the second commandment "like" the first?

Group Activities

1. On newsprint, whiteboard or chalkboard list the six actions named by Jesus in MATTHEW 25:35-36 as the basis for evaluating the authenticity of our faith. Brainstorm together and record the group's ideas on the board or newsprint. For each category, discuss:

   • Who are the people in our world today who need our service? in our community? in our families?

   • As a church community and as individuals, how are we serving Christ in these people?

   • What can we do better?

   • What steps can we take to start acting on our convictions?

2. Distribute paper and pencils. Ask group members to reflect quietly and begin making a list of their own talents. Use today's definition of talent, that is, gifts, abilities, skills. Reflect on the question, "What do I do well?"

   After a few minutes form groups of three or four and share the lists. Let small group members add to each other's lists additional gifts that they see in each other. Discuss:

   • How may each of these abilities be used to share Christ's love with others?

   Invite each group member to compose a prayer thanking God for his or her particular talents.

3. Distribute large sheets of paper and a variety of colored markers. Ask group members to close their eyes, relax and take a few deep breaths. Read MATTHEW 24:35 slowly, pause for a moment of silence, then read it again. Suggest that group members pay attention to the images that come to mind, and then each draw a picture or a symbol that illustrates the meaning of the passage. After a few minutes invite people to explain their images to the group.

4. In groups of three or four, write one sentence that summarizes Jesus' message in MATTHEW 24–25. Share these with the reassembled group.

Journal Meditation

Reflect on MATTHEW 25:34-46. Where in the ordinary course of your own life do you come into contact with hungry, thirsty, sick or imprisoned people? Think small. List the ways you respond to the human needs around you. Where do you encounter strangers? Who are they? What is your attitude toward them? What is your reaction to thinking of them as close relatives of Christ? as Christ himself? In your own words restate Jesus' final message to the disciples.

Stepstone To Prayer

Emmanuel, thank you for being with me in the sick, the needy and the lonely who cross my path each day. Help me to find you in yet others...

Matthew 26:1–27:26
The Last Supper, Arrest and Trial

CHAPTER 26 LAUNCHES the final portion of the gospel, the passion narrative for which all that precedes is preparation and through which chapters 1–25 must be understood. Without this part of the story Jesus would remain merely a wise, compassionate teacher and healer. Read MATTHEW 26:1–27:26.

Find The Facts

What celebration is about to occur in Jerusalem? What will happen to Jesus in conjunction with it? Who is plotting? Who agrees to deliver the victim? What happens between Jesus and the disciples as they gather for the Passover meal? What happens in Gethsemane? What is Peter's response? Who condemns Jesus to death?

1. List the characters that appear in this part of the passion story. Beside each name write a word or phrase that describes your sense of what the person is like.

2. With which of these characters do you most identify? Why?

Matthew 26:1-16

The first 16 verses of MATTHEW 26 serve as a prologue to the fast-paced narrative that follows. The addition of the word "all" to Matthew's familiar formula for concluding a discourse gives verse 1 particular emphasis. Jesus has now finished everything he has to say. As verse 2 states, the time is here to initiate the climactic action. While Jesus calmly states the time and manner of his death, the chief priests and elders plot nervously to bring it about. They agree the arrest must not be a public event. Jerusalem is crammed with people who have come to celebrate the Passover and a riot is a real possibility.

In nearby Bethany another kind of preparation takes place. Jesus is in the house of a leper (a legal outcast) when a woman performs an act of extravagant love. She pours a flask of expensive ointment on his head and, though the disciples protest the extravagance, Jesus calls her action a beautiful thing. Indeed it is the only anointing his body will receive before burial. (Note, *Messiah* means "anointed one.") Meanwhile, Judas solves the dilemma of the chief priests by offering to deliver Jesus to them. The plot against Jesus is now complete and Jesus himself is prepared for death.

Consider:

3. What significance do you see in the setting (house of Simon the leper) for the story of Jesus' anointing? How does it contrast with the setting for the dignitaries' plotting (vv. 3-5)? What light does this story shed on Jesus' description of the sheep and the goats in Matthew 25:31-46? In what way does the woman's generous response to the need she perceives relate to 25:31-46?

4. What motives might Judas have as he decides to collaborate with the chief priests? How do you think he feels when he accepts the money? How do you suppose he justifies his action?

Matthew 26:17-35

Passover, the great national feast of Israel, commemorates the establishment of Israel as the people of Yahweh through the reliving of the exodus story (Ex. 12:1-14). An important feature of the Passover celebration is the eating of matzo, unleavened bread that symbolized the haste in which the Israelites left Egypt. The feast of matzo was combined with an even older tradition of sacrificing the finest of the spring lambs in thanksgiving for God's bounty (Num. 18:17). In the exodus story, the blood of a sacrificed lamb smeared on the doorpost protected the lives of the first-born in the households of the captive Israelites. Still today, Jews and many Christians celebrate the story of deliverance and freedom through the Passover meal or Seder.

Thus on the first day of Unleavened Bread (Ex. 12:19-20) Jesus gives instructions for preparing for the traditional Passover meal. Passover lambs were sacrificed on this day at the temple, and in the evening the families gathered to share the meal. The Seder, though a religious feast, is celebrated in the home with members of the family. Jesus celebrates with those he has identified as his family (12:46-50).

The ancient ritual of the meal takes on dramatic new meaning for Christians when Jesus identifies his own body and blood with the bread and wine. The Jewish Passover commemorates the great saving event in Hebrew history; the new Passover is the saving person of Christ. In the

Old Testament, covenants are sealed by sacrifice (Ex. 24:8). Jesus becomes the new sacrifice for the new covenant.

Matthew frames the passage (vv. 26-28) that the Church calls the institution of the Eucharist by poignant forebodings of betrayal. Jesus, who knows human failings all too well, knows that Judas intends to betray him (vv. 20-25) and that the others will do so unintentionally (vv. 31-35). Even so, he symbolically breaks his body for them and shares with them his own life's blood.

Consider:

5. *How is your understanding of the Christian Eucharist enriched by seeing its roots in the Passover celebration—God's saving deliverance from slavery to freedom? From what and for what has Christ freed us? Where in your own life do you experience this freedom?*

6. *How do you feel when you think of Jesus' offering the model for our eucharistic celebration to those he knew would betray him? Describe the two kinds of betrayal Jesus predicts. Which is easier to cope with, deliberate, planned betrayal or the kind that happens in spite of good intentions? Describe a time when, in spite of your good intentions, you "fell away."*

Matthew 26:36-56

Immediately after the disciples echo Peter's earnest declaration of loyalty (26:35) comes the first falling away. Jesus takes the three disciples with whom he is most intimate to watch with him as he prays. We recall the themes of "watch, wait, be prepared" in the stories of the sleeping householder (24:42-44), the unprepared servant (24:45-51) and the slumbering maidens (25:1-13) as the disciples sleep through Jesus' agonized prayers.

Matthew portrays Jesus as profoundly human in this passage. Jesus shrinks from the approaching ordeal and prays to be delivered from it at the same time he seeks strength to do God's will. In verse 41, Jesus warns the disciples that they, too, will need to pray for strength to do what they intend to do (v. 35). They disregard the warning and, unprepared for the ordeal, flee when Jesus is arrested (v. 56).

Judas arrives on schedule, leading a group armed to arrest a dangerous criminal, and identifies the victim with the agreed upon signal. Jesus refuses to resist and points out that what is happening is necessary to fulfill the scriptures. Whatever happens he will obey.

Matthew presents Jesus as the supreme example of his own teaching. Jesus' prayer (v. 42) recalls the prayer he taught his disciples (6:10). He also taught love of enemies (5:44) and forbid any form of retaliation (5:39). He models this behavior now, surrounded by the violent crowd. As in the temptation in the wilderness (4:1-11) he rejects miraculous intervention (vv. 52-53) and submits to the angry mob.

7. What do Jesus' prayers in Gethsemane teach about prayer? How did praying help him in his struggle? Why do we need to pray? In your experience, when you are intensely troubled and your friends fall away, what strength and comfort come through prayer? What changes would you like to make in your prayer life?

8. What sort of response did the armed crowd expect from Jesus and his party? How do you think they felt when Jesus refused to fight? How did the disciple who tried to defend Jesus feel? Knowing yourself, how might you have reacted if you had been with Jesus when the armed crowd surged forward?

Matthew 26:57—27:2

Matthew describes Jesus' trial in three parts:

- a night session of the Sanhedrin in the high priest's palace (26:57-68)

- a brief morning session (27:1-2)

- the trial before Pilate (27:11-26)

The crowds take their prisoner to the palace of Caiaphas, the high priest, where members of the Sanhedrin are gathered (26:57). The Sanhedrin was the supreme court of Judaism and included scribes, Pharisees, Sadducees and elders of the people. The hearing proceeds swiftly with a series of false witnesses who fail to agree. Finally, two—the number required for valid testimony (DT. 19:15)—accuse Jesus of claiming power over the temple. Just as he refused to put up a physical defense, Jesus refuses to argue with his accusers. When he quotes DANIEL 7:13 (v. 63) the court condemns him for blasphemy. The penalty for blasphemy is death.

Meanwhile in the courtyard, Peter behaves as Jesus predicted. He denies any involvement with Jesus, not once, but three times, each more emphatic than the one before. As the cock crows, Peter recalls Jesus' words and, no doubt, his own response.

In the morning the Sanhedrin officially condemns Jesus to death and sends him to Pilate, the Roman governor who held office from A.D. 26-36. The governor was the one who had the authority to carry out capital punishment.

Consider:

9. *What do you think Peter is thinking as he follows Jesus to the palace? What conflicting emotions might he be experiencing? Why does he weep bitterly? In what ways can you identify with his conflict between his desire to follow Jesus and his instinct for self-preservation? See 26:41. How do you deal with such conflicts?*

10. How would members of the Sanhedrin expect one who claims to be the Messiah to behave? What kind of Messiah does Jesus' behavior suggest? What do you think of Jesus' method of dealing with his accusers? Does his silence indicate strength or weakness? Why?

Matthew 27:3-26

Another disciple besides Peter is nearby. Judas learns of the death verdict and regrets his actions. He tries to return the money and throws it down when the chief priests refuse to take it back. The despair Jesus had foreseen (26:24) overwhelms him.

The reaction of the chief priests and elders further demonstrates their hypocrisy. The ones who have privately perverted the justice system to condemn an innocent person to death are oddly scrupulous about use of the "blood money." They use it ostentatiously to do a public good deed. Matthew's account combines several Old Testament traditions from Zechariah (ZECH. 11:12-13) and Jeremiah (JER. 18:2-3; 32:6-15) to make his usual point that God's will is being fulfilled in all events surrounding the life and death of the Messiah.

The final portion of Jesus' trial takes place before Pontius Pilate. Jesus responds to Pilate's question with the same words he used before the Sanhedrin. His silence when accused by chief priests and elders puzzles Pilate who seeks to avoid making a decision by turning to the crowds. Custom apparently allowed the freeing of one prisoner during the feast of Passover, but the crowds choose Barabbas, not Jesus, for release. They roar approval of the Sanhedrin's recommendation of crucifixion for Jesus. In a final effort to avoid responsibility Pilate washes his hands, proclaiming his innocence in the affair. Such ritual washing of the hands was a Jewish custom (DT. 21:6), not a Roman one.

Consider:

11. *How do you feel about Pilate's final claim to innocence? How is avoiding participating in a decision similar to or different from actively taking one side or the other? In what way is this another example of "the spirit is willing, but the flesh is weak"?*

12. *Why do we have such different impressions of Peter and Judas, neither of whom behaved very admirably under pressure? What makes the difference? Why did one weep bitterly and the other give in to despair? In what ways do we demonstrate our loyalty to Jesus? In what ways, small or large, do we reject Jesus?*

Group Activities

1. Divide into groups of three or four and give each group paper and pencils. Ask groups to plan a television special of the events in this study. List the

characters you will include. How do you want them portrayed? Which ones will have major roles? Besides Jesus, is there a hero? a villain? How do your want your audience to react to them? What persons would you like to cast in the parts? Why?

Invite each small group to share its casting plan.

2. Ask group members to get comfortable, take a few deep breaths and close their eyes. Ask them to try to visualize the scene and place themselves in it as you read aloud the account of the trial before Pilate (27:11-26). Allow a few minutes of silence when you have finished reading. Suggest that each person turn to one other and share the answers to some of these questions.
   • Did you feel like one of the characters or an onlooker?
   • What did you visualize most clearly?
   • What feelings did you have?
   • What struck you as particularly significant or interesting?

   After a few minutes reassemble as a group and ask:
   • What are some new insights we have discovered through this exercise?

3. Jesus and the disciples gathered as a family to celebrate the Passover meal. In our society, what are some occasions when we gather with family and friends to celebrate with food and drink? List the responses on chalkboard, whiteboard or newsprint. In a parallel column, list special foods or drinks associated with the listed occasions, for example, turkey with Thanksgiving and cake with a wedding reception.

   Invite group members to brainstorm other ritual aspects of these occasions. Do they involve certain clothes? certain times of the year? In what ways do these special gatherings add meaning to our lives?

   In groups of two or three, discuss these questions about the Eucharist:
   • What are we recalling or reenacting when we eat the bread and drink the wine?
   • What makes the Eucharist a celebration?
   • How does the Eucharist add meaning to our lives? to our faith? to our relationships?

Journal Meditation

Twice in MATTHEW 26 (vv. 6-13, 17-29) Jesus takes time out from his journey to the cross to spend time in a domestic setting. What is the effect of these quiet interludes with friends? Remember these are the people that Jesus has identified as his true "family." Reflect on your own need for time out from your journey. What kinds of simple domestic gatherings or rituals strengthen you to continue?

Stepstone To Prayer

"Nevertheless, not as I will, but as thou wilt..."

Matthew 27:27–28:20
Crucifixion, Resurrection and Commission

THIS POWERFUL ACCOUNT of Jesus' crucifixion and resurrection presents the supreme paradox of the Christian faith, that One must give up his life so that others may live. Crucifixion (death) is necessary for resurrection (new life). In the final verses we receive our commission—to share this mysterious life-giving truth with all God's people. Read MATTHEW 27:27–28:20.

Find The Facts

How do the soldiers treat Jesus? What is the charge against him? What does Jesus say just before his death? Which friends stayed with Jesus till the end? Who made burial arrangements? Who discovered the empty tomb? What is Jesus' final word to us?

Consider:

1. *What emotions did you experience reading this story?*

2. *Where do you see yourself in the story?*

3. *What questions is the story asking you?*

Matthew 27:27-50

Scourging in order to weaken the prisoner was the usual preliminary to execution by crucifixion. After scourging Jesus (27:26), the soldiers take him into the praetorium, the official residence of the Roman governor who came to Jerusalem during the great feasts to help guard against riots. Here they stage a mockery, draping Jesus with pseudo-royal trappings. The thorns were most likely in the form of spikes radiating out from the head (like radiant crowns pictured on coins from the period). The crown of thorns also suggests the garland awarded to the victor in games. The reed represents a scepter, the symbol of ruling power. "Hail, King" corresponds to the greeting offered the emperor, "Hail, Caesar!" Ironically, the soldiers' sport proclaims the truth. As the reader knows, Jesus is King, not only of the Jews but also of those who mock him.

The execution then occurs according to usual practice. Crucifixion was a legal punishment until abolished by the Emperor Constantine (A.D. 306-337). The cross carried by Simon would have been only the crossbeam. The vertical stake was permanently sunk into the ground at the place of execution. Jewish custom allowed a narcotic drink to alleviate the pain of crucifixion, but Jesus refuses the sedative (v. 34). Prisoners were executed naked and their clothes given to the soldiers as a gratuity (v. 36). For the early Church the significance of verse 36 was the fulfilling of PSALM 22. A tablet stating the criminal's offense was commonly attached to the cross. Jesus' tablet bears a title—"King of the Jews"—and provides occasion for more mockery (vv. 37-44) from several groups.

Verse 40 recalls Satan's temptations (4:3) as an onlooker derisively hurls the ultimate temptation—"save yourself!"—at Jesus. But Jesus holds true to the decision he made in the wilderness (4:10). He demonstrates his power through loving service even unto death.

Matthew provides a dramatic setting for the end. Darkness, a biblical symbol for the end of the world (AMOS 8:9), settles on the land. In his agony Jesus cries out, using the words of the first verse of PSALM 22. The words express his sense of utter desolation and abandonment, a deeply human response. In the context of the entire psalm, which he might have been consciously quoting, the words are the prayer of a righteous sufferer who still trusts in God. Bystanders mistakenly believe he is calling for Elijah. According to the Old Testament account (2 KG. 2:9-12), Elijah did not die but was taken to heaven alive. One of the legends that grew out of Elijah's mysterious end says that he would come to rescue the righteous in times of need. So the Messiah dies in a supreme demonstration of obedience to God and love for humanity.

Consider:

4. *Matthew includes no description of Jesus' response to the soldiers' mockery. What, if anything, do you think he said? What might he have been thinking? When you feel put down or mocked how do you typically react? What gives you strength to tolerate such misunderstanding?*

5. *What three groups mock Jesus while he is dying on the cross? What is the significance of their insults? What would have been the outcome if Jesus had come down from the cross? Do you think he was genuinely tempted to do so? Why or why not? In what ways did his experience in the wilderness with the tempter prepare him for this moment?*

6. *Look up Psalm 22. Imagine Jesus praying this psalm in his last moments on the cross. How might it serve to express his deepest emotions? What sort of relationship does one who prays this prayer have with God? In which prayers do you find particular comfort in times of deep distress?*

Matthew 27:51-66

The Messiah dies amidst cataclysmic signs. The curtain which had screened access to the Holy of Holies (Ex. 26:31-35) in the temple rips apart, a powerful image of the new approach to God made available to all (Jew and Gentile) through Jesus' death. The earthquake emphasizes the cosmic dimensions of Jesus' death. The opening of tombs is another traditional sign of the beginning of a new age (EZEK. 37:12). For Matthew, the new age is here.

The reaction of the centurion and the soldiers in verse 54 is all the more dramatic because of their previous mocking unbelief (vv. 27-31). The exclamation of Christian belief from Gentiles is another reminder that Jesus is for all people. We may be surprised by who is able to see Christ most clearly.

The most faithful followers mentioned here are the women named in verses 55-56. They have come with Jesus from Galilee; they are present at the cross; they are there at the sepulcher for the burial. Such loyalty brings its own rewards: They are also the first to grasp the meaning of the empty tomb and the first apostles to unbelieving disciples (28:1-10).

A previously unknown disciple, Joseph of Arimathea, makes arrangements for an appropriate burial. Executed criminals normally were buried without honor in a public field.

Matthew wants to refute rumors (no doubt still circulating in the society of his time) that the claim of the resurrection is false. The centurion has been keeping watch at the cross to make sure Jesus dies; Pilate authorizes a guard at the tomb to prevent stealing of the body. After the resurrection, the chief priests and elders deliberately circulate a false report that the body is stolen (28:11-15).

Consider:

7. To Matthew, Jesus' death and resurrection have universal and cosmic implications. How does the death and resurrection of Jesus affect your view of history and the meaning of human life? How does it shape your understanding of the purpose of your life?

8. How would you describe the role of the women in this critical portion of the story? How do they stand in contrast to the jeering crowds? What does their presence at the cross and the burial site suggest? What qualities of discipleship are implied by their actions?

9. In what ways is the centurion's exclamation (v. 54) an answer to the challenges of the mockers in verses 39-44? Why do you think the Gentile soldiers were more receptive to Jesus than the leaders of the Church? What (besides the earthquake) do you think convinced the centurion that Jesus was the Son of God? What is the most convincing piece of evidence for you?

Matthew 28:1-15

Early Sunday morning the faithful women return to the tomb. Matthew dramatizes their experience through two impressive images, an earthquake and an angel. The earthquake is a favorite Old Testament symbol for a theophany, a manifestation of God. Angels are messengers from God (2:20). This angel comes to explain to Mary Magdalene and the other Mary (the mother of James and John) the meaning of the empty tomb and to give them a task. They must go quickly and tell the good news of Jesus' resurrection to the disciples. The scattered disciples should gather together in Galilee where Jesus will meet them.

As the women run to carry out their task they encounter Jesus himself. Their response is to hold and worship him. Before his arrest Jesus had predicted that all the disciples would fall away during the crisis (26:31-32). He also promised to reassemble them in Galilee after his resurrection. He repeats this promise now, generously referring to the scattered ones as brothers.

Verses 11-15 offer quite a different interpretation of the empty tomb. Just as the women have rushed off to find the disciples, some guards from the tomb recover from their fright and rush to report to the chief priests and elders. They agree to bribe the soldiers to say that the disciples came and stole the body while they were sleeping, not a very believable story, but evidently one still circulating in Matthew's time. Once again, the leaders are depicted as hypocrites, themselves guilty of the deception of which they accuse the disciples.

Consider:

10. What have the two Marys contributed to Christianity? Compare 28:3 with 24:27. Why do you think the two women were so receptive to the angel's message? How are they like the faithful servant (24:45-51) and the wise maidens (25:1-13) and unlike the unprepared householder (24:43-44)?

11. Which of the two versions of the empty tomb is more plausible? What kind of preparation does it take to enter into the experience of the two Marys and accept the version in 28:1-10? How do you explain your own belief in or experience of the resurrection?

Matthew 28:16-20

These last four verses draw together all the main themes of Matthew's gospel:

- Jesus as Messiah and Son of God

- Jesus as fulfillment of the law

- Jesus as the one who offers the promise to all

- Jesus as founder of the Church universal.

After the pivotal point of death and resurrection, Jesus comes with supreme authority to found and commission the Church. He meets the disciples on the mountain (compare 5:1 and 17:1) and entrusts them, worshipers and doubters alike, with a great task. He commissions them to go make disciples, baptize and teach. "In(to) the name" means "into the possession, protection and blessing of." Jesus' message and promise is not just for Jews, but for all people. Jesus, whose name is Emmanuel (1:23), promises to be with us always.

Consider:

12. *How do you fit into the Great Commission? What is one person's part in the task of making disciples of all people everywhere? Who invited you into discipleship? What gifts and insights can you offer to new disciples at this point in your life? (Remember that Jesus gave the task to all the disciples regardless of the certainty of their faith, v. 17.)*

13. *What does 28:20 mean to you? How does knowing God is with you impact your life? How do you share this impact with others?*

Group Activities

1. Divide into groups of three or four. Let each small group plan a skit or dialogue in which they explain the significance of Jesus' death and resurrection to a nonbeliever. Share these with the reassembled group.

2. Read aloud 28:16-20. Ask group members to try to imagine the feelings of the 11 disciples when they received the commission. Brainstorm quickly and record all responses on chalkboard, whiteboard or newsprint. Discuss:

   • Why do you think they felt that way?

   • How do you feel about this statement: "The task of disciples is to make new disciples"?

   • How well is the Church doing with this task? How does your own community understand its part in fulfilling the Great Commission?

3. Distribute paper and pencils. Ask group members to make notes while they reflect silently on four questions:
   - How has this study of the Gospel of Matthew changed your understanding of Jesus?
   - What new insights have you gained?
   - What new questions do you have?
   - How will you go about working on the answers?

   After a few minutes invite group members to share their reflections and new questions, noting them on chalkboard, whiteboard or newsprint.

4. Ask group members to listen from the perspective of the two Marys as you read MATTHEW 28:1-10 aloud.

   Distribute paper and pencils. Invite each group member to write a prayer that reflects the thoughts or emotions of these two women on the first Easter.

   Invite volunteers to share their compositions.

Focus on Matthew

Journal Meditation

Select a character found in MATTHEW 27:27–28:20 who interests you particularly. Reread the passages that mention this person (including those found elsewhere in MATTHEW). Imagine as many details as you can about this character. Enter into a conversation with the character by asking a question and imagining the answer. Write your dialogue down as quickly as you can. Be spontaneous—attention to spelling and grammar not allowed! Suggested opening questions: "What gift do you have for me?" "What do you want to teach me?"

Stepstone To Prayer

Jesus, truly you are the Son of God! Come near to me...Emmanuel.

Bibliography

Garland, David E. *Reading Matthew: A Literary and Theological Commentary on the First Gospel*. Macon, GA: Smyth & Helwys, 1999.

Hare, Douglas R. A. *Matthew* (Interpretation Commentaries). Louisville: John Knox, 1993.

Harrington, Daniel J. *The Gospel of Matthew* (Sacra Pagina). Collegeville, MN: The Liturgical Press, 1991.

Kingsbury, Jack Dean. *Matthew As Story*. Philadelphia: Fortress Press, 1986.

Luz, Ulrich. *The Theology of the Gospel of Matthew*. Cambridge: Cambridge University Press, 1995.

Overman, J. Andrew. *Church and Community in Crisis: The Gospel According to Matthew*. Valley Forge, PA: Trinity International Press, 1996.

Powell, Mark Allan. *God With Us: A Pastoral Theology of Matthew's Gospel*. Minneapolis: Fortress Press, 1995.

Senior, Donald. *The Gospel of Matthew* (Interpreting Biblical Texts Series). Nashville: Abingdon Press, 1997.

———. *The Passion of Jesus in the Gospel of Matthew*. Wilmington, DE: Michael Glazier, 1985 (now available through the Liturgical Press, Collegeville, MN).

Stanton, Graham N. *A Gospel for a New People: Studies in Matthew*. Edinburgh: T. & T. Clark, 1992.